Meeting the Needs of Children with Autistic Spectrum Disorders

9

Rita Jordan and Glenys Jones

David Fulton Publishers
London

David Fulton Publishers Ltd
Ormond House, 26–27 Boswell Street, London WC1N 3JZ

www.fultonpublishers.co.uk

First published in Great Britain by David Fulton Publishers 1999
Reprinted 1999, 2001

Note: The rights of Rita Jordan and Glenys Jones to be identified as the authors of this work
have been asserted by them in accordance with the Copyright, Designs and Patents Act 1988.

British Library Cataloguing in Publication Data
A catalogue record for this book is available from the British Library

ISBN 1–85346–582–8

Typeset by Textype Typesetters, Cambridge
Printed in Great Britain by The Cromwell Press Ltd, Trowbridge, Wilts.

Contents

Foreword

Each publication in this series of books is concerned with approaches to intervention with children with specific needs in mainstream schools. In this preface we provide a backdrop of general issues concerning special needs in mainstream schools. The government's recent Action Programme, published after considering responses to the Special Educational Needs (SEN) Green Paper, will lead to changes in practice in the future. Following consultation, there will be a revised and simplified Code of Practice in place by the school year 2000/2001. It is intended that this will make life easier.

The SEN Code of Practice (DfE 1994a), following the 1993 Education Act, provides practical guidance to LEAs and school governing bodies on their responsibilities towards pupils with SEN. Schools and LEAs were required to regard its recommendations from September 1994. The Department for Education also issued Circular 6/94 (DfE 1994b) which provided suggestions as to how schools should manage their special needs provision alongside that made by other local schools. These documents embody the twin strategies of individual pupil support and whole-school development. The Green Paper *Excellence for All* also seeks to promote the development of more sophisticated and comprehensive forms of regional and local planning (DfEE 1997).

The Code of Practice, with its staged approach to assessment supervised within each mainstream school by a teacher designated as Special Educational Needs Coordinator (SENCO), was widely welcomed.

For example, Walters (1994) argued that 'this Code of Practice builds on good practice developed over the ten years and heralds a "new deal" for children with special needs in the schools of England and Wales'. But he also reflected worries that, in the light of other developments, the process might provide an added incentive for schools to dump their 'problem children into the lap of the LEA' rather than devising strategies to improve behaviour in the school environment. Such children, he feared, were in danger of being increasingly marginalised.

Impact on teachers

While receiving a mainly positive welcome for its intentions, the Code of Practice (DfE 1994a) also raised some concerns about its impact on teachers who became responsible for its implementation. On the positive side the Code would raise the profile of special needs and establish a continuum of provision in mainstream schools. There was a clear specification of different types of special educational need and the Code's emphasis was on meeting them through individual programmes developed in cooperation with parents.

However, there were possible problems in meeting the challenge of establishing effective and time-efficient procedures for assessment and monitoring. Further challenges were to be found in making best use of resources and over-coming barriers to liaison with parents.

Anxieties about the Code

Following the introduction of the Code these anxieties were confirmed by a number of research studies of teachers' perceptions of the impact of the Code. The picture which emerged from these studies showed appreciation of the potential benefits of implementing the Code but widespread anxiety, based on early experience, about the practicalities of making it work.

Loxley and Bines (1995) interviewed head teachers and SENCOs about their views on emergent issues related to the complexities of introducing Individual Education Plans (IEPs), particularly in secondary schools.

Teachers feared that 'excessive proceduralism' could lead to the distribution of resources being skewed towards meeting the needs of children whose parents are best able to understand and exercise their rights, at the expense of provision for children whose parents are less assertive and confident. Teachers were most concerned about the allocation of scarce resources and the increased responsibilities of SENCOs for managing a system likely to reduce time for direct teaching of children.

School perspectives

Most schools were optimistic about their ability to implement the Code and positive about LEA guidelines and training, but there was less certainty that the Code would improve the education of pupils with SEN.

Asked to give their opinion on advantages and disadvantages of the Code, teachers cited as positive effects:

- a more structured framework,
- growing awareness of accountability,
- a higher profile for SEN issues,
- earlier identification,
- greater uniformity in practice, and
- increased parental involvement.

The disadvantages cited were:

- lack of resources and time,
- substantially increased workloads for all teachers as well as SENCOs,
- more time used for liaison and less for teaching.

(Rhodes, 1996)

Four themes

A national survey commissioned by the National Union of Teachers (NUT) identified four themes:

1. broad support for the principles and establishment of the Code of Practice;
2. concern about the feasibility of its implementation, given a lack of time and resources;
3. problems in some areas related to perceived inadequacy of LEA support;
4. inadequate status and lack of recognition for the SENCO role.

(Lewis et al., 1996)

Another study found patchy support for SENCOs. There were wide variations in the amount of time dedicated to the role, the amount of support from head teachers and governors, involvement in decision-making, the extent of training and the degree of bureaucracy within LEAs.

SEN Register and Staged Assessment Procedures

Although its widespread adoption makes it appear to have been a national prescription, the five-stage model suggested in the Code is not a legal requirement. The Code actually states that: 'to give specific help to children who have special educational needs, schools should adopt a staged response'. (DFE 1994a, 2.20)

It goes on to indicate that some schools and LEAs may adopt different models but that, while it was not essential that there should be five stages, it was essential that there should be differentiation between the stages, aimed at matching action taken to the pupil's needs at each stage.

Five Key Stages

Nonetheless, the normal expectation is that assessment and intervention will be organised and recorded in an SEN Register for which the SENCO is responsible. The following description briefly summarises usual practice, with Stages 1-3 school-based and Stages 4 and 5 the responsibility of the LEA.

Stage 1
Class teacher identifies pupils with learning difficulty and, with support from the SENCO, attempts to meet the pupil's SEN.
Stage 2
Class teacher reports continued concern and SENCO takes responsibility for the special response to meet the pupil's SEN.

Stage 3
SENCO organises support from external agencies to help in meeting the pupil's SEN.

Stage 4
The LEA is approached by the school with a request for statutory assessment.

Stage 5
The LEA considers the need for a Statement of SEN and completes the assessment procedure; monitoring and review of the statement is organised by the LEA.

Each book in this series, explains how this process works in relation to different disabilities and difficulties as they were described in the 1981 Act and shows how individual needs can be identified and met through IEPs. While forthcoming revision of the Code may alter the details of the stages, the principles of the practices through which needs are specified will remain the same.

Information for colleagues, governors and parents

Ensuring that the school provides all necessary information for staff, governors and parents is another major element of the SENCO role. *The Organisation of Special Educational Provision* (Circular 6/94) (DfE 1994b) sets out the issues which the school should address about its SEN provision, policies and partnerships with bodies beyond the school.

This is information that must be made available and may be found in school brochures or prospectuses, in annual reports to parents and in policy documents. The ultimate responsibility for following the guidance in the Circular rests with the head teacher and governing body but the SENCO will be engaged with all these issues and the Circular forms in effect a useful checklist for monitoring the development and implementation of the SEN policy.

You may find it useful to consider the following points as a way of familiarising yourself with provision in your school.

Basic information about the school's special educational provision

- Who is responsible for co-ordinating the day-to-day provision of education for pupils with SEN at your school (whether or not the person is known as the SEN Co-ordinator)?

- Arrangements need to be made for coordinating the provision of education for pupils with SEN. Does your school's SENCO work alone or is there a coordinating or support team?
- What are the admission arrangements for pupils with SEN who do not have a statement and is there any priority for SEN admissions?
- What kind of provision does your school have for the special educational needs in which it specialises?
- What are your school's access arrangements for pupils with physical and sensory disabilities?

Information about the school's policies for the identification, assessment and provision for all pupils with SEN

- What is your school policy on allocation of money for SEN resources?
- How are pupils with SEN identified and their needs determined and reviewed? How are parents told about this?
- What does your school policy say about arrangements for providing access for pupils with SEN to a balanced and broadly-based curriculum (including the National Curriculum)?
- What does your school policy say about 'integration arrangements'? How do pupils with SEN engage in the activities of the school together with pupils who do not have special educational needs.
- How does your school demonstrate the effective implementation of its SEN policy? How does the governing body evaluate the success of the education which is provided at the school for pupils with SEN?
- What are the arrangements made by the governing body relating to the treatment of complaints from parents of pupils with SEN concerning the provision made at the school?
- What are your school's' time targets' for response to complaints?

Information about the school's staffing policies and partnership with bodies beyond the school

- What is your school's policy on continuing in-service professional training for staff in relation to special educational needs?
- What are your school's arrangements regarding the use of teachers and facilities from outside the school, including links with support services for special educational needs?
- What is the role played by the parents of pupils with SEN? Is there a 'close working, relationship'?
- Do you have any links with other schools, including special schools, and is there provision made for the transition of pupils with SEN between schools or between the school and the next stage of life or education?

- How well does 'liaison and information exchange' work in your school, e.g. Links with health services, social services and educational welfare services and any voluntary organisations which work on behalf of children with SEN?

In any school those arrangements which are generally available to meet children's learning needs will have an impact on those services which are required to meet specific needs. It is therefore very important that a reader of any one of this series of specialist books makes reference to the general situation in their school when thinking about ways of improving the learning situation for pupils.

Harry Daniels and Colin Smith
University of Birmingham
February 1999

References

Crowther, D., Dyson, A. *et al.* (1997) *Implementation of the Code of Practice: The Role of the Special Educational Needs Co-ordinator.* Special Needs Research Centre, Department of Education, University of Newcastle upon Tyne.

Department for Education (DfE) (1994a) *Code of Practice on the Identification and Assessment of Special Educational Needs.* London: HMSO.

Department for Education (DfE) (1994b) *The Organisation of Special Educational Provision.* Circular 6/94. London: HMSO.

Department for Education and Employment (DfEE) (1997) *Excellence for All: Meeting Special Educational Needs.* London: HMSO.

Hornby, G. (1995) 'The Code of Practice: boon or burden', *British Journal of Special Education* 22(3) 116–119.

Lewis, A., Neill, S. R. St J., Campbell, R. J. (1996) *The Implementation of the Code of Practice in Primary and Secondary School: A National Survey of the Perceptions of Special Educational Needs Co-ordinators.* The University of Warwick.

Loxley, A. and Bines, H. (1995) 'Implementing the Code of Practice: professional responses', *Support for Learning* 10(4) 185-189.

Rhodes, L. W. (1996) 'Code of Practice: first impressions', *Special!* Spring, 1996.

Walters, B. (1994) *Management of Special Needs.* London: Cassell.

CHAPTER 1

Introduction to autistic spectrum disorders

Diagnoses and labels

The isolation of autism need not be a negative trait ... We don't deserve to be condemned or laughed at, or made to fit into the plastic box of society's correctness. We shouldn't spend our entire lives trying to become someone else, someone acceptable ... It is unfair to be continuously labelled, analysed, picked to bits, dissected like a specimen, peered at with a large eye through a magnifying glass.

(O'Neill 1998, p. 199)

The quotation above is from a person with an autistic spectrum disorder (ASD) and reflects the growing trend (in common with other people with disabilities) for people with autistic spectrum disorders to assert their right to be different. This sometimes seems at odds with the views of parents and professionals that an early diagnosis is crucial for providing effective services, including education. In fact the views are complementary, not opposed. Teachers (and others in a teaching role whom we will refer to as 'teachers' for convenience, regardless of their professional designation) need to recognise the differences if they are to ensure that a pupil is to develop fully and is not to be handicapped by the misunderstandings and misinterpretations of behaviour that will otherwise follow.

A medical diagnosis is not the sole determiner of a special educational need, yet it may be a necessary precursor to providing the support that will prevent a pupil developing such a need. It is not a question of 'to label' or 'not to label'. We all naturally categorise and give labels to people, based on the behaviour we see, and it is a matter of a diagnosis helping us to interpret the behaviour in ways that are helpful, rather than misleading and discriminatory. A pupil may be described as 'lazy', 'rude', 'aggressive' and so on. These 'labels' will then partly determine how we react to the behaviour. A diagnostic label, however, alerts us to the fact that there may be other less obvious reasons for the behaviour, which in turn will lead to more appropriate and helpful reactions. Pupils with autistic spectrum disorders are still individuals, of course, and there are reasons why they may in fact be more different from one another than other pupils; knowing that a pupil has such a disorder does not tell you exactly how they will behave or exactly how they should be taught. A young man with Asperger's syndrome put it very well:

Autism is not a label; it is a signpost. (Exley 1995: personal communication)

We hope that this book will help those working with pupils with autistic spectrum disorders in mainstream settings reach some understanding of that signpost.

'Autistic spectrum disorder' is the name given to a family of biologically based disorders which comprise a number of different medically diagnosed conditions. There are two different diagnostic systems which may be used for these diagnoses, which have slightly different criteria and classification but share a common understanding of the features that must be present; one of these is the International Classification of Diseases-10 (ICD-10: World Health Organisation 1992) and the other the Diagnostic and Statistical Manual-IV (DSM-IV: American Psychiatric Association 1994).

The diagnostic categories that fall within these two systems and which we are calling autistic spectrum disorders (after Wing 1996) include:

autism
autistic disorder
atypical autism
Rett's syndrome
childhood disintegrative disorder
Asperger's syndrome
pervasive developmental disorder
pervasive developmental disorder, not otherwise specified
semantic pragmatic disorder

Sometimes, people making the diagnosis, especially if it is made in connection with defining a pupil's special educational needs for a statement or record of needs, will use other less-defined descriptions. For example, a child may be described as having 'autistic features', 'autistic traits' or even 'autistic tendencies'. Such terms do not have any validity, as we discuss below, but generally indicate that the person making the diagnosis may be unsure or feel that the full diagnostic criteria for any of the list of disorders given above are not met, yet the child still appears to have 'autistic' difficulties.

Semantic pragmatic disorder was often used before the diagnosis of Asperger's syndrome became common and it will still be used by some professionals, mainly speech and language therapists. It indicates that a child has good structural language skills but has some difficulties with meaning and with understanding how language is used in social contexts. Everyone with an ASD who has speech will have semantic and pragmatic difficulties; the question is whether there are individuals who just have those difficulties and do not have the social and flexibility difficulties that make up the underlying triad of impairments that characterise an ASD. Most research suggests that children with semantic pragmatic disorders do have these additional characteristics, albeit in a mild and subtle form. From a practical standpoint, it is usually helpful to treat them as if they had an ASD in any case.

A large proportion of pupils with autistic spectrum disorders have additional learning difficulties, some severe. Those with Asperger's syndrome or 'high functioning autism' will not have general learning difficulties and may in fact be very intellectually able or even gifted in certain areas, but even so this group may still have additional specific difficulties such as dyslexia. Nor is there anything in autism that protects a child from having additional sensory or physical difficulties. Older children and young adults may also develop mental illnesses (just as other people do) and may have specific reasons for depressive illnesses, related to their growing awareness of their difference from others and the lack of peer support that usually aids the difficult transition from childhood to adulthood. Teachers of that age group will need to be aware of this additional vulnerability and the need for extra support at this time.

The difficulties in learning that are a direct result of the autistic spectrum disorder are better characterised as 'differences', since they only become difficulties if they are not accommodated. Within the constraints of mainstream settings, this can be difficult at times, although not impossible. This book aims to help staff understand the perspective of a pupil with an autistic spectrum disorder and to encourage schools to accommodate their differences. Flexibility is required when a pupil is experiencing problems in understanding what is required or in following the usual conventions within school. On a good day, those challenges are stimulating and teaching pupils with autistic spectrum disorders can be fulfilling and fun. On a bad day, the teacher may feel it is all too difficult, that he or she is making too many mistakes and that the pupil would be better off in a specialist situation. Occasionally that is true, but there are no magic solutions, even for those who have gained specific expertise in working with such pupils. A commitment to the pupil and a recognition of his or her right to as inclusive an education as possible, is an important step in meeting their needs. All teachers should recognise that everyone makes mistakes when working with children with autistic spectrum disorders, because they require ways of reacting that do not always fit what seems natural or how we would react to others; the only secret is to recognise those mistakes and learn from them.

The basis of autistic spectrum disorders

The shared characteristics of all autistic spectrum disorders have come to be known as the 'triad of impairments' (Wing 1988) although, as explained in the preceding paragraph, they might be better characterised as developmental differences rather than impairments. Each diagnosis includes criteria related to these three areas of development. Note that they represent developmental areas, rather than specific behaviours. There are no behaviours that are of themselves characteristic of autism (that is why it is misleading to speak of 'autistic features/traits' and nonsensical to speak of 'autistic tendencies') and it is necessary to have 'impairments' in all three areas before a diagnosis can be made. Autistic spectrum disorders are more easily characterised by aspects of development that are missing or abnormally delayed, but the way the pupil's behaviour reflects these developmental difficulties will vary from one individual to another. These individual differences reflect the interrelation with other difficulties or strengths, the child's personality, his or her experiences, and the particular setting being considered. There will not only be differences between individuals but also over time within the same individual.

Social interaction: This is the most obvious and characteristic area of difference, but even so there will be great individual variation. Some pupils may show the classical features of being very socially withdrawn and isolated, relating neither to adults nor peers. Others may be very dependent on familiar adults, especially parents, and may join in passively with familiar children such as siblings, but have difficulty initiating social contact with others and making friends. Even more common in mainstream settings will be those pupils who appear very sociable, in that they seek contact and may try to dominate contact with both adults and peers, yet cannot manage to get that interaction right and appear socially awkward and naive. It is not just that friendship behaviour is absent or disturbed, however, but that they do not understand social signals and find it difficult to learn through the social interactions that are characteristic of most kinds of learning situations in schools.

Communication: Although language difficulties are commonly associated with autistic spectrum disorders, most of the pupils who are in mainstream settings will not have obvious difficulties with spoken language. Autistic spectrum disorders are the only cases, however, where structural aspects of language (its grammar and articulation) may develop without an underlying understanding of communication. Regardless of language ability, pupils with autistic spectrum disorders will have problems using language to communicate or understanding how others do so. They tend to interpret language literally and never go beyond that to take into account what the speaker was likely to have meant.

All but the most obvious facial expressions and communicative gestures are either not attended to or are seen as puzzling distractions. Intonation can be heard (as witnessed by those children who echo exactly what they have heard, maintaining the original intonation pattern) but the pupil usually cannot understand the meaning that the intonation pattern conveys. Generally, even in those pupils who are dominating interactions with long monologues, there are difficulties in engaging in conversations and in processing verbal information (especially when utterances are long or spoken rapidly); their own level of language use is a poor indicator of the language level they can process and understand.

Flexible thinking and behaviour: Sometimes 'imagination' difficulties are referred to in this area, but that can be misleading. Pupils with autism in mainstream settings do have difficulty in creating something entirely from their imagination but that does not mean that they cannot be good and even exceptional artists in the visual, musical or even language arts. They also do not join with others in the typical shared pretend play situations of early childhood but they may show an ability to 'imagine' within their own narrow play routines; it is with sharing in the imagination of others and creating joint play scenarios that they have most difficulty. More important for their daily learning experiences, they have difficulty abstracting central meaning (especially social or cultural meaning) from their experiences, generalising learning to new situations, problem solving outside of cued rote responses and broadening interests to other than a few narrow (often obsessional) ones that dominate their thinking and behaviour.

Range of provision

Whether or not a mainstream teacher will encounter pupils with any of the autistic spectrum disorders depends almost as much on government and local educational policy as it does on the features of the actual disorders. It also depends on the age-range and context. Thus, it is still often policy in many areas to include children in mainstream settings at the pre-school level, almost as a form of assessment, and only later send some to specialist (autism specific) or special schools or units. Mainstream schools in rural areas may need to include a wider range of pupils than areas where there are sufficient children to form units or resource bases. It is not possible to say that one form of provision is the best for all pupils with autistic spectrum disorders; child and school characteristics as well as parental wishes will help determine the best setting for each individual (Jordan and Powell 1995a).

Table 1.1 gives some of the pros and cons that are associated with mainstream placement, although these can only be broad generalisations, given the enormous variation within the mainstream sector. It should also be remembered that the 'ideal' placement for a particular pupil may change over time. It is our view that children with autism would benefit most from early specialist education within which the child can develop the skills needed to learn in less specialised settings at a later date (Jordan and Powell 1995b, Jordan and Jones 1996).

With increasing emphasis on inclusion, and growing awareness of autistic spectrum disorders among all professionals, this does not necessarily mean that that specialised teaching needs to take place in segregated specialist settings and certainly it should become rare for a child with an autistic spectrum disorder to spend all of their educational life in segregated settings. There may be early segregation to teach initial skills but even then, mainstream teachers should become increasingly involved in staged integration experiences for these pupils. Later on, at adolescence or early adulthood, there may again be a need for some students to move to specialist settings for residential provision to teach independence skills and

Table 1.1:   Pros and cons of mainstream placement for children with autistic spectrum disorders

Pros	Cons
1. Access to 'better' models of social and linguistic behaviour.	1. Many staff and pupils to be understood and adjusted to.
2. Easier access to full curriculum resources including the National Curriculum.	2. Curriculum may not be designed to meet the special needs of the pupil.
3. Specialist subject teaching to develop child's interests and strengths.	3. Less likelihood of staff having knowledge of autistic spectrum disorders.
4. Peers available as a resource for 'buddies' and teaching aides.	4. Poorer staff:pupil ratio to identify and meet needs and develop skills, except when extra adult support is allocated.
5. Higher expectations to develop knowledge and skills and improve life chances.	5. Less realistic expectations and less availability of curriculum methods that reduce stress and enable learning.
6. Broader opportunities for curriculum development, qualifications and career choice.	6. Fewer opportunities to learn in functional contexts and to address difficulties that interfere with life chances.
7. Locational opportunity for social integration within a community and for family involvement.	7. Poorer understanding of isolating effects of the disorder and fewer resources to support families.
8. Opportunities to spread awareness and tolerance of ASD in society.	8. Fewer opportunities for staff to share problems/experiences/successes with others and gain support.
9. A better context for developing understanding of, and conformity to, the cultural values and rules of society.	9. Assumptions of 'normality' as a framework offer less understanding and tolerance of difference.

to aid the difficult transition to adult life. The movement across specialist and mainstream settings should be more a matter of planned progression rather than exclusion; the direction of the process should generally be from the specialist towards the less specialist rather than the reverse.

Case studies

The following are examples of pupils and young adults who have been or are being educated in mainstream settings. They represent examples only, not necessarily typical of the way an autistic spectrum disorder may be displayed by another child with the same disorder, or of the same age. Each case is unique. They have been chosen to illustrate the range of abilities that may be found in pupils with an ASD in mainstream settings and how their different needs can be accommodated to make the placement a success.

Amy: a three year old with autism and learning difficulties in a mainstream nursery

At three years old, Amy was a delightful little girl with blonde curls and a ready giggle. She was very appealing both to staff and other children but her failure to join in with their games and to grab and pull their hair was already making most of them lose interest and shun her. Left to herself, she would flit from one activity to the next, sometimes picking up items and mouthing them, sometimes sweeping the entire contents off the table onto the floor. The more distress and anger her behaviour produced, the more amused she appeared to become and this infuriated both children and staff.

Amy ran most of the time, rather than walked, with a tiptoes gait, but there was no occupational or physiotherapy advice available to the staff to explain what this meant in terms of motor development or to help with exercises and management to overcome these difficulties. She was still drinking from a bottle when she came to the nursery at 2.5 years but staff had weaned her onto drinking from a cup, although she still needed supervision to ensure she did not throw it. She did not speak, although she did 'sing' and used speech sounds in that context. Nor did she respond to spoken instructions, although she had been taught successfully to respond to her name and she enjoyed lap games with staff, especially involving tickling, and chasing games with staff or other children.

She was particularly responsive to music and the only time she would sit quietly was to listen to instrumental music (especially live music). A peripatetic music therapist visited the group and staff were taught to develop turn-taking with her in the context of music making, and this was successful.

The open plan arrangement and loose structure of the nursery did not suit Amy and staff realised that they would need to impose some structure if she was to concentrate and learn. A period each day of one to one learning was established in a corner of the room, separated from the general 'confusion' by a screen. Within that arrangement, Amy learnt a number of table-top activities (drawing lines with a pencil, recognising her written name, threading beads, labelling items in a book, sorting objects by categories and doing simple inset puzzles) and remained able to concentrate for a period of 20 minutes. The rest of the time she was 'shadowed' by staff to avoid problems and assisted to join in with others. She learnt to participate in simple social games with other children but only where music was involved to provide a structure she understood.

A review at four years showed that she had made considerable progress in many areas but she was not developing speech nor learning to play with others (two of the main reasons for admission to the mainstream nursery). Staff were advised on how to encourage her to communicate clearly with them and Amy was taught to request what she wanted from staff and her parents using the Picture Exchange Communication System (Bondy and Frost 1994). Both staff and her parents created opportunities throughout the day where she needed to communicate to get what she wanted. Strategies which encouraged her to play alongside other children and engage in short turn-taking games with them were also adopted. She continued to require close supervision when she moved into the reception class and was given periods of individual teaching to work on communication and other skills.

James: a seven year old with autism in a primary school

James is a seven year old boy with autism. He had entered a small village primary school at the age of five, without any formal diagnosis of his condition. He had displayed difficulties in developing language and social development which had led to his referral to a speech and language therapist at the age of three. Autism had not been mentioned to the parents and they had attributed the difficulties they were experiencing in managing his behaviour and engaging with James, to his difficulties in developing speech. They thought that once he developed speech he would no longer get frustrated and could tell them what was the matter. They also felt that would solve his difficulties in relating to other children.

By five, however, although he had developed speech and was talking fluently, he still did not seem to listen and could not engage in conversation, and his behaviour and social problems seemed to be getting worse rather than better. A formal assessment of his educational needs was sought and a medical diagnosis of autism was obtained when he was nearly six. As a result of the diagnosis, and the extent of his special educational needs, a statement was issued which gave James 15 hours a week from a special support assistant. The person appointed (who had experience of supporting other children with special needs in mainstream, but not autistic spectrum disorders) remained with James throughout his time at the school. The local authority did not have training courses for such staff nor any outreach support teachers in autism, but they paid for both the teacher and the support assistant to attend some day courses in autism and, through the parents, the teachers made contact with the local autistic society who were able to offer information and practical advice.

At seven, James was able to keep up with most of the academic work he was given, although he relied on his support assistant to explain what he was to do and to structure his time and keep him 'on task'. Playtimes and dinner time were a problem for staff as James had not learnt how to play with other children (nor they with him). His support assistant was not available then as she took her break at the same time. James was often trying to get back into the school at these times and use the computer or hide himself behind the bench in the cloakroom. Even more worryingly, he would be bullied or teased by the other children and would exacerbate these problems by lashing out when they came near him. Nor would he accept punishments or even admonition; he would walk away when the Headteacher was talking to him and had kicked the dinner lady who was trying to prevent him entering the school during the lunch break.

His support assistant was asked to take her break slightly earlier and to support James during the playtimes. A circle of friends was created for James to develop his ability to play effectively with them and to work successfully with a partner in classroom activities. In the early weeks of the circle's formation, the support assistant was on hand to prompt or assist, but eventually the children developed their own strategies and she was no longer required.

Ahmed: a 15 year old with Asperger syndrome in a mainstream school

Ahmed did not receive a diagnosis until he was 14 years old. He had been a difficult child, but he had developed speech early, had been a prodigious talker and developed special interests in dinosaurs and then geology and his 'oddness' was thought to result from superior intelligence and the fact that there was a four year gap between him and the youngest of his five brothers and sisters. His parents were first generation immigrants from the Indian sub-continent and their culture discouraged the seeking of outside help for what were regarded as 'family' matters. Even after diagnosis, the parents did not belong to any parental society for autism and their concerns at school meetings were with Ahmed's academic progress rather than the implications of his disorder. The school suspected that Ahmed was presenting behaviour problems at home but the only time this was discussed was in relation to an incident when Ahmed had been 'arrested' for shoplifting and the school's help was sought in explaining the behaviour to the police.

The school was in an urban setting within an authority that had a specialist advisory teacher for autistic spectrum disorders and provided peripatetic support and training for staff in mainstream schools. It was because of this support in relation to another pupil that Ahmed's difficulties were first recognised by the school and diagnosis sought. Following diagnosis and a review of Ahmed's needs, a dual system was instituted. In the academic subjects at which he excelled he was accelerated and allowed to take GCSEs a year early. He was also allowed to pursue some of his more esoteric interests to an even higher level to enrich his learning, through computer assisted learning and access to a geology class held at a local college of further education. This required the motivation for him to develop some of the social skills he needed to participate in this latter setting, and he was encouraged to identify his own missing or poorly developed skills and to develop his own programme for working on these.

In addition, a circle of friends (Taylor 1997, Whitaker *et al.* 1998) was established to support him at school, especially in breaks and less structured periods. As a development from this, some 'special buddies' were identified who helped him with his difficulties in organising himself to move from lesson to lesson and to understand the requirements of the set homework. His skill with certain subjects, and in his use of computer technology, was drawn on to show him that he too could help others. In that way he increased in self-esteem and was able to develop some relationships with his peers. He still had occasional difficulties but strategies were developed (e.g. social stories) for him to prepare for new or stressful situations and also to reflect on and learn from past problems. He completed his schooling in mainstream and currently attends university on an accountancy and business administration course with the goal of working within his family business.

CHAPTER 2

Language and communication – problems and strategies

The range of the difficulties

Autism itself does not lead directly to problems in structural language development, although there may be associated specific language difficulties and/or difficulties in acquiring language that come from additional severe learning difficulties. Occasionally, a facility for acquiring language (a first language and additional second or foreign languages) is an area of strength in an individual with an autistic spectrum disorder, but it is more common for there to be problems with this area of learning. By definition, those with Asperger's syndrome will have developed language at a normal or near normal age but those with autism (even if high functioning) are usually delayed in their acquisition of spoken language and continue to have relative difficulties with verbal aspects of learning and expression compared to other aspects of development.

If a child does not develop speech, or has limited speech for his or her mental age, then parents and teachers are alerted to the fact that the child has difficulties and are more likely to make allowance for those difficulties in their interactions with the pupil. If, however, teachers are confronted by a pupil with fluent speech, who never seems to stop talking, it is unlikely that they will recognise that the child has a problem in processing speech, or has a problem in understanding communication, and are equally unlikely to make allowances for those difficulties when interacting with that child. Thus, an apparent facility with spoken language may mask a child's true difficulties and delay, or even prevent, him or her from gaining the support he or she needs.

The nature of communication

In order to understand the range of these problems and how they may be dealt with in practice, it is necessary to understand the difference between language and communication. Language is often defined as a system of communication, but autistic spectrum disorders show how language may develop divorced from its role in communication. Other children may have difficulties in acquiring spoken language and, to the extent that that is so, their communicative ability may be limited, but they will do their best to compensate by communicating through alternatives such as gesture and mime. Children with ASDs, however, are the only group who may develop spoken language skills in advance of, and often in the absence of, the ability to communicate. Those who do not develop speech, likewise, do not compensate through gesture or mime and have great difficulty in understanding such communicative attempts.

In order to communicate, one needs:

- communicative intent;
- something to communicate about;
- a means for communicating;
- a reason for communicating.

Children with an ASD typically lack communicative intent, although they learn ways of making requests or protesting, to get their needs met. They do not spontaneously monitor the eye direction of others (although they can look where someone is looking or pointing if they are directed to do so) so they do not establish joint attention with others. As babies, and even later, they do not automatically direct their attention to things that are held up for them or pointed out through eye-gaze, pointing, or the use of deictic language (e.g. 'here' versus 'there', 'my' versus 'your' etc.). This leads to a range of problems such as semantic difficulties (through not understanding what aspect of the environment is being labelled), lack of awareness of being addressed, or knowing how to address others, and problems with personal pronouns (thinking that 'you' or 'he/she' always refers to the self because they have heard others use it in reference to themselves).

Although pupils with an ASD have the full range of emotional experiences, often have very good rote memories especially for facts, and are able to think about a range of things (according to cognitive ability), they may not have conscious awareness of their own mental processes. Thus, they may know things but not know they know them until that knowledge is triggered in some way. They may feel afraid or angry but cannot communicate that emotion because they are unable to reflect upon it. In addition, their lack of awareness of shared knowledge or experience or the separateness of their own mental processes from those of others, means that they cannot gauge what their listener needs to be told or what is redundant; in consequence, their speech is either over pedantic (making explicit information which would normally be implicit or shared) or ambiguous (failing to supply the relevant context and assuming that the other person has access to the same information as oneself, even if they have not had an opportunity to share that experience).

It is easier to understand when children with an ASD have problems with the means of communication. Except for nursery provision, there are not many children with an ASD without language (spoken or alternative) in mainstream settings. However, in situations where the mainstream teacher is involved in helping the child develop language, it is important to be aware of the difficulties specific to autism that may be encountered. Sign language may be almost as difficult as speech, and photographs, pictures, symbols or written words may be the best route through to developing speech.

Finally, an autistic spectrum disorder may also give rise to problems in the reason for communicating. If children's communicative attempts are not recognised, then motivation to communicate is lessened and this can happen in children with an ASD because they may not use conventional ways to communicate and their consequent idiosyncratic attempts are not recognised. This, in turn, may lead to the child giving up on communication and resorting to former successful ways of getting his or her own way. Equally, there also needs to be some 'pressure' to communicate. This 'pressure' is absent, if all of a child's needs are anticipated, as can sometimes happen when parents are anxious to avoid the mayhem that results when, for example, a child's favourite video is not ready to play when he comes home from school, or the breakfast cereal is not ready on the table in the morning. The term 'pressure' is not used here to mean that the child should be pressurised into using words or his or her best form of communication, but to argue that opportunities to communicate should be created and provided by the staff.

Conversational difficulties

Pupils with an ASD have difficulty in recognising the topic of conversations, in knowing how to introduce their own topic without causing conversational failure, and how to maintain and extend topics. They also have difficulty in knowing how to draw conversations to a close, without being abrupt or even rude. Even when they have managed some of these skills, they find timing of conversations very difficult and are often interrupting others or leaving uncomfortable pauses because they cannot predict when pauses are coming nor recognise when it is their turn and when they should relinquish the floor to someone else. Finally, they are not well motivated to listen to the contribution of others and seek to turn conversational exchanges into monologues on their own concerns. They also find it easier to hold the floor than to actively listen and monitor the contribution of others. This skill can develop over time, however, often with explicit teaching.

Early conversational skills can be developed but it is increasingly difficult to develop the higher skills that lead to conversational fluency and timing. Pupils can be taught turn-taking by teaching children to hold a conch (or a microphone, if preferred) while talking, and then to pass it on to others for their turn. They can be taught to listen to stories and pick out the topic through acting it out with puppets as it is told. They can be taught to listen and take account of the contribution of others through a game whereby there is an object on which a small group take turns to comment, each child being required to make a comment that is different to that made by the others. They can be taught to listen to others by learning to interview them and to ask further questions based on the answers given. All these are useful precursors to conversational ability, but putting them together in meaningful contexts with appropriate timing eludes all but the most able pupils with an ASD. After mastering the basic skills, practice seems to be the best way of improving performance.

Limited communicative functions

Problem: The young child with an ASD, even in a mainstream school, may not have developed any communicative intent or may only use his or her language for a very narrow range of communicative functions. Typically, they will make requests, protest, and expound upon favourite topics, irrespective of the relevance to the communicative situation or the interest or communicative needs of their 'audience'. They rarely use language to direct the attention of others, to comment on the environment, to provide knowledge for others, or to seek knowledge from others. They may well answer questions but their responses to questions are triggered by those questions and they do not work out or volunteer information that someone else might need. Similarly, they may ask questions, and even do so obsessively, but this has other purposes than the communicative one.

Approach: The very young child who needs to develop his or her understanding of communication itself, and how to express communicative intent, is best approached through the communicative function of request. Situations should be engineered so that the child cannot simply get the desired object for themselves, but needs to ask for it in some way. If the object is available and the child is just made to ask for it, he or she will not learn about communication but just that this is some ritual that they have to go through in order to get what they want (i.e. they will learn about conformity and politeness, which may be valuable lessons but do nothing to clarify communication). This means that in a nursery school, for example, all materials and toys should not always be available for the child's free choice; instead they may be placed on high shelves or in inaccessible cupboards but with labels at child height so that the children can use those labels to make their requests.

In asking, children need to be taught that just saying certain words (or using certain signs symbols or gestures) is not in itself sufficient. They may mutter or whisper their requests or make requests to an empty room. They have to be taught to gain people's attention (in socially acceptable ways according to the status of the person involved) and to delay their communication until they have gained this.

Older or less affected pupils may understand about simple communicative functions but need to learn how to share information and comment on their environment. Rather than expecting the pupil to learn to do this in situations that have no meaning for them, it is best for the adult to start with an activity that the pupil enjoys. They may need specific prompting from the teacher, for example, to point out relevant aspects of a computer display to another pupil with whom they are 'sharing' a computer task. When they are doing something they enjoy, it can be brought to their attention explicitly by being told that they are enjoying it and, furthermore, that their parents are at home or at work and do not know that they are doing this. Then they can be reminded before they go home of what they have done and that they should tell their parents about this because their parents do not know about it. Parents can be phoned (or there can be a word with the parent who collects the child from school) to prime them to ask initially about the specific activity, but later to ask a question the child has been taught to answer such as 'What did you do in school today?' Many normally developing children may not be able or willing to answer such questions, but it is only the child with an ASD that will need specific teaching how to do so.

Example: Mary was an able 4.5 year old with autism, entering the reception class of a mainstream primary school. She had always been very independent in meeting her own needs and her parents had encouraged her in this. In addition, her mother had learnt the kinds of things that Mary wanted and the times she wanted them and, to avoid the outbursts of frustrated anger that would otherwise erupt, she organised that these things were readily available at the relevant times. Mary had attended a mainstream nursery where activities were made available from which the children could choose and Mary spent her time there 'choosing' the same favourite activities. She did learn to say 'biscuit please' in response to the set question 'What do you want?' at snack times, but it was clear that this was learnt as a set routine that had little to do with communication.

In the more formal reception class there were more set activities but with free-time toys and materials in a cupboard to which only the staff had free access. Even in activities that were set up for the children, the materials were available for the group, rather than for an individual. Mary was making herself very unpopular by grabbing materials from other children and apparently ignoring the requests of others to give or pass them things. For other children this might have been simply an inability to share (and clearly this was something Mary needed to learn to do as well) but for Mary there was also the problem of not understanding the need to communicate nor to recognise the communicative attempts of others. An example of this was when the teacher intervened on behalf of another child, whose attempts to get Mary to pass her the yellow paint were being ignored. 'Mary, can you pass Bridget the yellow paint please?' said the teacher. 'Yes,' replied Mary (who answered direct questions or commands as long as her name was used and the command was not just addressed to the class or group as a whole) but without passing the paint.

Having recognised the problem and not attributed Mary's behaviour to rudeness or selfishness, the teacher instituted a programme to help Mary ask for things explicitly. In free play times, for example, where she had previously been at a loss and often interfered with others by destroying what they were doing or taking their things, Mary was given a picture 'menu' of the free-time activities and materials that she could choose from. She was taught to find a member of staff, to wait if they were talking to someone else, and, having gained their attention, to ask for one of the items on her 'menu'. She was also taught to recognise and respond to the requests of others (both issued as direct commands and then as more polite indirect commands) in graded steps, starting with role play situations with adults and then moving to prompted situations with other children. Each step needed to be taught in explicit detail but, once Mary had grasped what was required, her behaviour was transformed and her relationships with the other children greatly improved.

Literal understanding of language

Problem: Pupils with an ASD interpret language literally, not understanding the implications that may be drawn, the way the meaning may be changed by the way something is said or the accompanying gestures and/or facial expressions or what the speaker intends to say. They will not understand indirect commands if they are phrased as questions, nor use context or common sense to work out what was meant, and they have problems with non-literal aspects of language such as sarcasm, metaphor, irony or idioms. Children with an ASD have been known to be terrified, for example, when told that someone is 'crying their eyes out' or when asked by a nurse in a hospital (the child having some partial knowledge of the kinds of things that go on in hospitals) to 'give me your arm'. They may react to commands to wipe their feet on the mat by taking off their shoes and socks to do so and, although this may be amusing for the onlooker, it is a clear indication of how confusing language can be for even the most linguistically able child with autism; plus it illustrates the many opportunities there are for teasing and bullying by others.

English itself is a very metaphorical language, although our normal skill in interpreting the intention behind the literal message hides this from us until we are sensitised through the reactions of the child with an ASD. Young and less able children with an ASD may even be reluctant to accept synonyms or homonyms. Many will be unable to make the cause of their confusion and distress explicit and so this will often require detective work. A girl with autism, for example, was screeching and biting her hand but it was proving difficult to understand what was leading to this behaviour. Then, watching a videotape of a classroom session, it suddenly became clear that the trigger in each case was someone apparently saying 'no', which she associated with frustration and prohibition. It had been hard to pick up in the actual situation because some of the supposed 'no's' were in fact 'know's' to which she attributed the same adverse meaning. Nor, of course had she been able to differentiate the 'no' addressed to her from that addressed to others.

Approach: It would be impossible to avoid the use of non-literal language in mainstream settings. The emphasis, therefore, must lie in recognising the many possible causes of confusion and distress and developing a programme to help the child understand these non-literal forms of language. Pupils with an ASD will need practice through videotapes, role plays and specific guidance in actual situations, in recognising the different ways of conveying the same meaning and the different meanings that may be conveyed by the same language in different contexts or with different expressions and tones of voice. Because it will be impossible to teach every idiom or synonym, the aim should be to illustrate the ways in which meaning is determined apart from, although including, the actual language used. Then there needs to be another programme to teach the pupil to express his or her confusion (by a simple phrase such as 'I don't understand') without getting upset or displaying unwanted behavioural reactions.

It may seem that this will present an intolerable amount of effort for the mainstream teacher but many of the aspects of the teaching can be done in class contexts which will benefit all. Thus, other pupils (especially those for whom English is a second language) will benefit from this explicit teaching of meaning through language and all children will have their language understanding, and through that their linguistic expression, enriched.

Example: George was a ten year old with autism with good structural language skills and an advanced reading ability, but an extreme intolerance of non-literal language forms. There were numerous examples of his failure to draw normal implications from what he heard such as when told to take the register to the office, taking it but bringing it back again because he had not been told explicitly to leave it there or give it to someone. He was constantly in trouble because he appeared to be disobedient or defiant. For example, he might be told to 'watch where you are putting your feet!' as he clumsily trod over art work laid out on the floor to dry, only to enrage the member of staff as he deliberately trod on the piece of work while carefully watching his own feet with interest. Another typical example was when a parent helper in the class asked him if he would like to come and read to her only to be told, very politely, 'No thanks!'

But the most disruptive effect of this disability was his intolerance of synonyms and homonyms. He would get enraged when such terms were used and shout 'wrong words!' at the top of his voice, sometimes also throwing things or banging his head on the desk. This reaction alerted the staff to the cause, but it was too difficult to eliminate the use of such terms. Instead he was given numerous exercises to do in school and for his homework in which he was taught to identify such terms, to look up synonyms for words in a thesaurus and to work through and discuss a book of cartoons that illustrated in a humorous way (although he often had to be taught to recognise the humour) the literal meaning of idiomatic phrases. To give a flavour of this, the cover of the book was a picture of a young boy with his hand in a pool of vomit; the caption was 'Tom was feeling sick'. 'Poor taste' greetings cards are often a good source of further resources that can be used.

After several months of this programme, George's behaviour improved dramatically and he became noticeably less tense in English lessons. There were still many things he did not understand and there was little generalisation from one idiom to another. Yet a useful by-product was that he began to understand jokes as well (since it had been necessary to teach these as part of the programme) and even to make up his own. These were rather painful for the adults around but not markedly more so than those of other ten year old boys and the other children proved an appreciative audience. This further encouraged him to make up these 'jokes', gave him a certain status among his peers and through that enabled him to develop friendship groups for break times.

Repetitive questioning

Problem: Many children with an ASD do not understand or use what linguists call the 'sincere' purpose of questions: the finding out of information that is not already known. Instead they use questions for other purposes, many of which they see modelled in teachers' uses of questioning. Pupils with an ASD may repeatedly ask the same question in what appears to be an obsessive way and do not stop when told the same answer or told that they already know the answer. In desperation, teachers adopt strategies for limiting the questions either by restricting the number of times a question may be asked or the time period in which such questions are permitted. Neither of these strategies is very successful, with the pupil becoming increasingly anxious and unable to concentrate on other work and often culminating in the breakdown of the prohibition.

Approach: As with all challenging behaviour in autism, the first step is to try to understand it from the pupil's point of view. It is unlikely that the child is doing it just to be annoying, although, if that is a predictable response in a largely unpredictable world, the regular display of annoyance may come to be rewarding. Nor is it likely, given the child's difficulty in understanding mental states, that the purpose is to find out information (i.e. that it is a sincere question). Thus it will simply mystify the child to be told 'you already know the answer to that'. To understand, one needs to look at other purposes for questions.

Within educational discourse, teachers will continue to use the same question until the 'correct' (i.e. the 'intended') answer is given. The pupil with autism will hear the different intonation pattern of the teacher's 'yes' in response to answers that are right in fact, but are not what the teacher intends, and the 'yes' that signals (to the rest of the class) that the intended answer has been given and the repetitive questioning can stop; he or she can hear the different intonation patterns but they cannot attribute meaning to them. As far as such pupils are concerned the teacher arbitrarily asks the same question several times and then arbitrarily stops. Likewise, teachers will frequently ask questions to which they patently know the answers, with the intention (not perceived by the pupil with an ASD) of finding out, not the answer, but whether the pupils know the answer: display questions in fact. Once again, such experience makes it very puzzling for the pupil to be told 'you know the answer to that' as a reason for not asking the question.

In times of anxiety everyone may ask repetitive questions, hoping to receive the same answer to relieve their anxiety; the obvious example is the question 'do you love me?' hoping for the same answer 'yes, of course I do'. The more anxious we are, the more likely we are to repetitively ask this question, to seek the reassurance of the same answer. Or we may have recently been told that our loved one loves us and in our besotted joy we ask that same question again and again just for the pleasure of hearing the same answer.

The reasons for repetitive questioning in pupils with an ASD, then, may be that they are following a model of questioning that they regularly see in their teachers, that they are expressing anxiety and seeking reassurance or that they are enjoying hearing the 'set' answer to that question (if only because it is 'set' and therefore predictable). The first thing then is not to further confuse with apparently irrelevant comments but to try to determine what purpose is being served in this instance. Once that is determined, teach the pupil alternative ways of achieving the same end. If it is simply copying, the pupil should be taught to understand the teacher's purposes in asking questions through explicit teaching. If the pupil is anxious then the source of the anxiety must be acknowledged and the pupil given other strategies for dealing with that anxiety and getting reassurance. If it is just that the pupil wants to hear the answer then make sure the pupil has other strategies for introducing and maintaining favourite topics of 'conversation', although there may still need to be some time constraints on this until the child has developed more conversational skills. Finally, the pupil will also need explicit teaching of the sincere purpose of questions.

Example: Stuart was a 17 year old with Asperger syndrome who was attending vocational courses in computer studies at a college of further education. He had no problems coping with the academic part of his courses and funding had been obtained for support during the lunch break and for someone to escort him and teach him to use public transport, with a view to his future independent travel. Stuart enjoyed his lunch time paid 'companion' because this was a fellow student whom Stuart regarded as a friend. However, he was still anxious about all the uncertainties of public transport and very dependent on the woman who came to escort him. His anxiety was further increased when the bus she travelled on to the college broke down one day and she was an hour late in meeting him. Ever since that occasion, Stuart began to ask everyone, almost as soon as he arrived, if Lucy was coming to take him on the bus. He would interrupt lessons to ask, and drive his lunch time companion crazy with his repetitive asking. This had got so bad that the young man was thinking of giving up the buddying 'job'. This would have been a further blow to Stuart's security and so a specialist counsellor was asked to work on a programme to help Stuart with his anxiety over the transport arrangements and to give him another way of expressing it.

The programme had several parts. The anxiety was tackled first by getting Stuart to produce (using his computer) a daily timetable in which each period was clearly marked, both with what Stuart would be doing and with whom he would be doing it. When he asked about Lucy coming, he was not answered directly, but directed to this timetable where Lucy's arrival was clearly noted. In addition he was taught to confront his fears through coping strategies for the feared situation of Lucy failing to arrive to pick him up. Strategies included instructions of how long to wait, and what to do then, including a flow chart that made the options explicit. Because of his love of mathematics, Stuart was encouraged to work out the chances of a further bus breakdown based on past bus statistics. All this decreased his anxiety and allowed him to concentrate on his travel independence programme, further decreasing his anxiety as his confidence in his own ability increased.

CHAPTER 3

Developing social relationships

The difficulty in teaching social skills

Social interaction difficulties are at the heart of autistic spectrum disorders but the range of social behaviour shown in children with an ASD is vast. As with any developmental disorder, the behaviours seen are not just a reflection of inborn characteristics but of how that individual has compensated for any initial difficulty and, conversely, how that initial difficulty may have led to further difficulties in development. In autistic spectrum disorders, it is notable that the initial difficulty in recognising and giving appropriate social signals may result in exclusion from the very social situations that are needed for further social development. Thus, the difficulty can become a handicap, unless intervention can prevent these secondary difficulties from developing.

Yet the fundamental nature of the social difficulty means that it is not simply a matter of identifying and teaching missing social skills. Nor does mere exposure to social situations enable the child with an ASD to pick up and respond to social signals; if it were that easy, the child would not have the problem in the first place. As able people with autism have noted (Sinclair 1992, Williams 1996, Gerland 1997), it is not enough to get them to copy 'normal' social behaviour without any understanding of what they are doing. Not only is this extremely stressful and difficult for the person with the ASD, but it does not enable them to generalise these behaviours to other situations (or at least it does not guarantee that if they do try to do so the result will be appropriate or correctly timed), nor to adapt them as the situation changes. It is the prime feature of social behaviours that they are flexible and finely attuned to changing social situations. Trying to teach social skills without the responsiveness and understanding that normally underpins them, often just results in making children appear even more socially odd as they stick to learnt routines that are no longer adequate.

There is even the danger that teaching social skills, without the necessary understanding and consequent adaptability, may result in increased vulnerability in the child with an ASD. If children are taught, for example, to look at people when being addressed, without understanding why they are looking, or how to time and modify their gaze, then they may end up staring unblinkingly and unnervingly into people's eyes. Apart from appearing uncomfortable and unnatural, such behaviour may well be interpreted as being provocative of either a sexual advance or aggression, those being the only two situations in which it is common to stare into another's eyes. Either of these interpretations are liable to make the person vulnerable.

Similarly, teaching confident ways of entering social situations through teaching greetings and the initial moves of a social exchange (small talk, for example), without ensuring that subsequent skills are in place, may mean that the pupil's initial behaviour misleads those he or she is interacting with into false assumptions about that individual's social competence. Thus, there will be no support offered and subsequent social failure may be interpreted as deliberate rudeness or worse. Teaching must always ensure that the pupil is not encouraged to enter into relationships without the necessary skills and experience to manage them.

Thus, the approach should be one of enabling the pupil to gain appropriate and rewarding social experiences and making rules underlying social behaviour explicit. Apart from the ineffectiveness and dangers in an approach of teaching to deficits, there is also the problem of motivation. Identifying a pupil's problems with social interaction and devising a programme to remedy them is likely to be rejected by the pupil with an ASD, who may not recognise these as 'problems' or 'deficits' nor be well motivated to 'work on them'. It is better to wait until the individual has a social goal such as wanting a friend, or a job and then to use an analysis of the skills needed to achieve that goal to introduce the idea of the social skills that will also need to be acquired. Alternatively, able pupils may be helped to identify their own problems and devise their own programmes for dealing with their difficulties (Barber 1996).

Enabling learning in social situations

Problem: There are two aspects to this problem. On the one hand there is the problem of being able to learn through social mediation (i.e. from a teacher, using social strategies such as demonstration and discussion) and on the other there is the problem of being able to learn in a group situation. At the lowest level, the pupil must be able to tolerate sitting near to others, having others sit near to him or her and must be aware that he or she is part of a group so that group instructions and rules are recognised as being applicable to the self. At the highest level, the pupil should be able to learn through group interaction, problem solving together and learning from group discussion and the sharing of ideas. The goals in the latter list may be too ambitious for most pupils with an ASD, but the lower level skills should be attainable by nearly all the pupils with autistic spectrum disorders in mainstream schools.

Approach: Gradual toleration of the presence of others in the classroom should start with the level at which the pupil is comfortable and able to concentrate, even if this means that a separate space in the classroom is devised at first. This might be in a corner, with a screen on the third side and the pupil's single desk as a barrier to others, as the pupil sits either facing the wall or with their back to the wall. Schools with individual desks in rows are hard to find now in the UK, but they represent an almost ideal situation for children at this stage in their social development. Group teaching with pupils sharing tables in open plan settings represent the worst conditions for such children and few children with an ASD will be able to learn in such a setting unless it is gradually introduced and the pupil's need for personal clearly marked space is respected.

Pupils with an ASD will also need explicit teaching to recognise that they are part of groups (the class) or sub-groups (boys, the blue group, those who did maths yesterday and so on) and an initial strategy of using the pupil's name as well as the group address (e.g. everyone and Sarah get your coats; girls and Sarah line up over here) can be faded, once the pupil is used to doing what the others do and recognising the existence of sub-groups. To begin with, pupils with an ASD should not have their academic progress hindered by forcing learning through social mediation. If pupils can learn by themselves either by structuring the presentation of the materials or through computer assisted learning, then this should be permitted, as long as a programme for social learning is also in place.

Learning to learn in social groups should first be attempted through tasks which are already familiar, so that the pupil with an ASD is learning to do the task with others while the others may be concentrating on the task itself. New skills may first be taught through one to one teaching with an adult, but the pupil should then be given the opportunity to practise these in group settings. Even where a support assistant is available for the pupil with an ASD, that support should not always be in the form of direct teaching, but also in enabling the pupil to interact with, and learn from, other pupils. Peer tutoring can also be used to help structure the interaction between other pupils and the pupil with the ASD and this may also help the other pupils get to know and understand the pupil with the ASD. Research shows that children in such tutoring roles benefit as much as the child they are helping, so there are no ethical problems in adopting this strategy.

Example: Alex was a five year old boy with autism in a reception class of 33 other children and with only 40 minutes support a day from a special needs teacher (not specifically trained or experienced in ASD). The 'classroom' was part of an open plan setting whereby the same noise and activity areas were shared by another reception class of 33 children and a nursery class of 20 children. There were tables set out for group work with eight children seated round each table for 'quiet' work. All periods were characterised by a continuous traffic of children to and from the different activity areas and the noise of other children 'working', playing or being instructed.

Faced with this confusion of noise and social activity, Alex initially retreated underneath a table, with his ears covered by his hands and violently resisted all attempts to move him. After a while, he could be coaxed out to sit for short periods with the table pushed against a wall and with the teacher on his other side. But even in this position, he was clearly in a constant state of anxiety and unable to concentrate. He continually flinched as children passed by and repeatedly aligned and realigned his ruler, pencil and paper as the activity of the classroom caused them to be dislodged. Eventually, in spite of some disapproval voiced by the head teacher, the class teacher got the rest of the class to build a little 'house' for Alex out of floor bricks. A small table and chair were placed inside and for the first time he was able to concentrate and learn. He did not spend all day in the house and other children were allowed time in the 'house' so that it did not completely separate Alex from the group.

Once Alex was secure in his house, it was brought nearer and nearer to the other children working, until he was virtually seated at one end of their table, but surrounded by three walls of his house. The next step was to gradually take down the house, a brick at a time and each time keeping at the stage at which he was still comfortable and able to work without distress. It took six months for Alex to learn to sit with the others round a table without excess anxiety and without flinching.

Developing friendship groups

Problem: Pupils with an ASD vary in the extent to which they wish to make friends and mix with others. They also vary over time. Some children, at puberty, develop an interest in others and in having friends. However, even if a pupil expresses hostility to the notion of having friends or mixing with others, this cannot simply be accepted at face value. In the pupil's long-term interests, the teacher needs to ensure that this reluctance to mix with others and develop friends does not result from fear or lack of experience. We cannot claim that a pupil is making a meaningful choice to be on his or her own until we are sure that the individual has all the necessary skills to form and maintain friendships and has some direct experiences to give meaning to the notion of what a friend is, and the possibilities that may arise from friendships.

Approach: Developing friendships is not only important for its own sake, but because it opens up support networks that help prevent teasing and bullying by others. This in turn will help reduce the need for adult supervision at all break times, although 'friends' may continue to need adult support for their role (perhaps through a 'circle of friends' teacher-facilitated support group) if they are to continue. Friends also make better teachers of how to play (Roeyers 1995) than do adults and they are the only ones who can help the adolescent move from dependence on adult oriented rules to an adult role of making one's own choices and developing one's own code of conduct. This may be an unrealistic level of independent functioning to expect most pupils with an ASD to reach, but the aim of using peers as a reference group when choosing clothes or deciding on leisure pursuits should be achievable and can be fostered by personal and social education while at school.

Pupils with an ASD (especially those with Asperger's syndrome) often restrict their interests in interacting with others to those that are deemed to be the most powerful; they reject other pupils in favour of the support assistant, reject him or her in favour of the teacher, reject the teacher in favour of the head teacher and so on, according to availability. One way round this is to devolve some power downwards, at least in situations that are important to the child with the ASD. Thus other pupils can be put in charge of a timetable controlling access to computer time, or determining the video to watch on a wet playtime. Even better than putting a single pupil in charge, is to insist on consensus decisions for certain events, while ensuring that the pupil is first taught the debating and assertive skills necessary to participate in making such decisions.

The more enjoyable the events that are shared with others, the more the pupil with an ASD will get to know such children in relaxed circumstances and the friendlier he or she will be able to be with them. If the pupil enjoys an activity such as swimming, then teachers should look for ways of making this a group, rather than a solitary, activity. Working at the computer is another such example and also deals with the danger that the pupil may develop an obsessive interest in the computer that makes them even less likely to mix with others.

Example: Faisal was an 11 year old boy with autism in the top year of a junior school in a city area that had a policy of full inclusion. He had had the support of an assistant for ten hours a week and there were weekly visits to the school by the outreach teacher for autism. The support assistant was taught to prompt Faisal to attend to instructions from the teacher and to support him during the unstructured times at break and dinner times, rather than working directly with him herself. This had worked well in that it had enabled Faisal to access the curriculum for his academic subjects without the continual barrier of a support assistant between him and the other pupils and he had made good progress in most academic subjects. However, he had never learnt to interact with the other pupils at break times. Attempts had been made, supported by the assistant, but they became less successful as the pupils got older and their interests changed. At a review meeting, worries were expressed about the transition to secondary school and the way in which Faisal was becoming more rather than less isolated from the other pupils just at a time when he was becoming interested in having friends for the first time.

In analysing what had changed, it was apparent that the dominant playground activities were now strongly gender based and represented activities that were distinct weaknesses for Faisal. The boys almost exclusively played or talked about football and the girls just talked and laughed, mainly about clothes, boys and broken friendships. When they were younger the children had been prepared to include Faisal (prompted by the support assistant) in their more eclectic and less divided games; they had even been willing to learn new games or adjust their games to include him. But, because he had had the support assistant, Faisal had never had any particular buddies and now none of the pupils were sufficiently committed to him to risk losing their own important social circle. Nor was Faisal able to join in either of the two major activities. The girls did not want a boy in their group and in any case he could not engage in the kind of informal banter and gossip in which they were engaged. The boys were not prepared to tolerate someone who could not seem to remember whose side he was on, who was poor at directional kicking and was completely unable to hold on to the ball or pass it if he was tackled; he just 'froze'. The solution of allowing him to play with younger children was tried but Faisal was very large for his age and clumsy and tended to frighten the younger children; in any case it did not solve the problem of the imminent transition.

It was decided to teach Faisal how to be a better football player and to enlist the support of his male peers in a circle of friends to develop strategies for doing this. As a result of a suggestion at one of these meetings, Faisal was tried in goal (on the grounds that he would have a clearer task and would not be tackled in the same way) but this failed because he found it difficult to keep 'on task' and to respond quickly enough as the ball came towards him. In the end the efforts to teach him football were not very successful in improving his performance, but they were successful in gaining the sympathy and even empathy of the other boys and they eventually came up with the solution. In the process of trying to make Faisal better at playing football, he had been taught all the rules of the game and how to recognise fouls and so on. The boys suggested he become the unofficial referee of their games and this was accepted because he was seen as impartial and not tied into friendship groups on either side. They also argued less with him, perhaps because they now recognised his vulnerability or perhaps because he was actually impartial. He also had status and became much more relaxed about the prospect of changing schools 'with his mates'.

Teasing and bullying

Problem: The difficulties experienced by pupils with an ASD in understanding others and knowing how to react to them in ways that are not seen as odd, means that such children are very vulnerable to teasing and even bullying. At certain times, for certain children, their desire to have friends may lead them to do anything that will gain approval from their peers. Thus, they can be 'set up' by other pupils to do naughty or even dangerous things and, because of their naivety, they will have little idea of the consequences of their actions or how to lie to protect themselves. Not only are they usually 'caught' or will own up when asked, but they will also tell on others, because they do not understand concepts such as loyalty or the balancing of one rule (you must answer the teacher's question) against another (you must not tell on your 'friends'). This may then lead to further bullying and to further bewilderment and fear for the individual.

Approach: Having a 'buddy' scheme for playtimes and breaks can help as both protection and for teaching the pupil with an ASD ways of interacting more successfully with others. Creating a circle of friends can also be used in the same way if the pupil gives his consent to this. Initially, the pupil with the ASD and his or her circle discuss how he or she might be included in their work and leisure activities. Particular pupils plan to sit next to them for certain activities or to partner them in PE or to go to lunch with them. Other pupils in the class who observe the circle also observe how they might relate to the pupil with the ASD and may start to do this naturally, without prompting. It is important also to involve parents for the child's fear and anxiety may be being masked at school but it will usually show first at home, as it does for other children. Thus parents can warn the school of situations that are developing before they become too difficult to change.

Once a child has developed a full school phobia it may be impossible to retrieve the situation at that school. Although it is important that a school has an anti-bullying policy and all cases need to be addressed for the sake of the emotional and social development of all pupils, it is important also to remember that the pupil with the ASD is not just a victim. There is usually something that the child is doing, or failing to do, that has been the immediate trigger and it is important to address that as well, rather than relying on others to become more empathetic and kind for any sustained period.

Example: Aaron was a 14 year old with Asperger's syndrome who was developing school phobia because he said he had no friends and the other pupils bullied and teased him, especially at break times. He was an only child who lived with his mother who was now finding it impossible to get him to go to school in the morning and had turned to her social worker for help. Aaron was an able child who had only received a diagnosis in the previous year. The SENCO had little knowledge of ASDs but was very experienced in dealing with a range of other special needs where instances of school phobia and bullying often arose. She was detailed to work with the form tutor and the mother to develop a strategy for this situation.

To start, she visited Aaron at home and listened to his complaints against the other pupils and empathised with his fear of going to school. But then she produced a detailed and specific contract which both she and he were to sign which confirmed that he would agree to come to school for a month and she would arrange to protect him from bullying during that time and to develop strategies with him that could be agreed for the next contract. At school, Aaron was allowed to use a computer during the long lunch break but she accompanied him in the shorter breaks to observe the behaviour he complained about. She tried to make herself inconspicuous, by talking to other staff, but to begin with other pupils avoided Aaron while she was there. This was in fact helpful at this point since it reduced Aaron's fear and helped him manage the short breaks, but after a while the pupils accommodated to the SENCO's presence and more usual behaviour reasserted itself.

From her observations, it became clear to the SENCO that there was indeed a fairly high level of teasing and low level bullying going on, but that Aaron was by no means the sole or even the prime target for this. The situation changed from day to day with respect to targets, but most pupils seemed to come in for a turn as target. Yet there was a difference in the interactions with Aaron. With other 'victims' the other pupils seemed to develop a good feel for when they had 'gone too far' and they would quickly revert to placatory moves to re-establish friendship; they would say things like 'only joking mate' and give a friendly punch, or pretend cuff round the head, followed by an arm round the shoulder and so on. But when Aaron was the target, he reacted differently to begin with and his sudden (and sometimes vicious) retaliation caught them off guard so that they escalated the conflict rather than going into placatory mode. Even if they tried the same placatory moves that they used with other pupils, however, Aaron did not recognise the intended placatory intention and saw them as a continuation of the bullying. He then reacted to that and the situation soon got out of hand.

Thus, there needed to be two aspects to the programme instituted. On the one hand the form teacher was supported by the SENCO in running anti-bullying workshops for all the class in which different vulnerabilities were exposed and the special difficulties of several of the children, including Aaron, were discussed. The class group came up with and role played various strategies for managing difficult situations and making intentions clearer for Aaron. They also accepted that they would need to modify their behaviour to accommodate Aaron's needs and that this was the strong, not the weak, thing to do. This took several months to work through and implement but improved general break-time behaviour for all of the pupils. Aaron's form won the prize at the end of the year for the form that had made the best contribution to the life of the school, as a result of the implementation of that programme.

At the same time as he was taking part in this form programme, Aaron was also having individual sessions with the SENCO where he was taught (through the analysis of television soap episodes, which he really enjoyed) more about the meaning of certain interactions and reactions, including the kinds of behaviour that he had falsely identified as aggressive and bullying. He was helped to generalise this to the actual situation by the role plays with his form mates and by prompts from the SENCO who continued to spend time with him in breaks, on an intermittent basis. There were other incidents in the future but overall the programme was a great success, not least because it enabled Aaron to participate in and learn from the social exchanges he needed.

CHAPTER 4

Helping the children become more flexible

Special needs that arise from a lack of flexibility

Social and communication difficulties largely affect the context of learning, at least at school, but difficulties in being flexible have a profound effect on learning itself. The effects of inflexible thinking that have been noted include problems in attending to relevant aspects of a problem or changing focus to accommodate changes in a task. Memory is extensive in terms of rote learning but pupils with ASDs need cues to retrieve their personal memories (e.g. to recall what they did yesterday, at the weekend, last lesson) and they cannot recall the gist of what has happened. In the same way they can learn lists of facts but do not seem to connect them with existing knowledge patterns or even to be aware of what they know, until it is cued. They tend to learn set routines and even set responses to questions, which they cannot modify and become upset if required to do so. Interrupted while they are in the process of a monologue on some area of interest, they cannot start again from where they left off but need to go back to the beginning. Skills learnt in one situation do not generalise to new situations unless this is specifically taught.

Because so much of their behaviour is triggered by the environment, children with ASDs are at a loss in new situations or when their normal response is blocked or ineffectual. They can be creative in a craft sense, and produce very aesthetically pleasing work in music, visual arts or even movement. Yet the work is almost invariably based on what that person has seen or been taught in the past; it does not come entirely from the imagination although parts may be combined in new original ways. There is a young talented artist with autism in France who has made literally hundreds of accurate and fascinating drawings of a futuristic city that he has invented. His scale drawings show a city with new combinations of buildings but each of the buildings are of themselves, or contain elements of, buildings that he has seen and enjoyed from around the world. There is the Taj Mahal, the pyramid from the Louvre, buildings from Barcelona and the Eiffel tower, for example. Each night, the young man puts a compass into his plan of the city at random and then makes another drawing from the perspective of that direction. All the drawings are consistent and the whole is a wonderful example of creative, but not entirely imaginative, intelligence.

At more basic levels, children with ASDs either do not engage in pretend play at all or play very rigidly with toys and do not extend or accommodate their play to involve anyone else. Creative writing tends to follow taught patterns of how to write or reflects the style of the books the child reads. Mechanical and geometric aspects of mathematics are often strengths, but the child may have problems with estimation and prediction and relating learnt strategies in calculation to real world situations. Science subjects also may be strengths, but it is categorisation, tables and chemical formulae that they are attracted to rather than the process of hypothesis testing. The National Curriculum emphasis on communication and discussion as a way of problem solving and disseminating findings has been disastrous for many children with ASDs, turning a successful subject into one which is now problematic. Teaching needs to take account of these difficulties by allowing greater flexibility in the presentation of results.

Choice is always a difficulty since it requires the child to hold two alternatives in mind at the same time. The child with an ASD finds it hard to consider alternatives or to make a decision when the possibilities are open. Thus, there are problems in deciding what to do in unstructured situations, in answering open-ended questions and in inhibiting one action when the alternative action is not prescribed.

Improving flexibility

There are specific areas of thinking that can be developed, as the sections below suggest. But, overall, it should be remembered that rigidity in thinking in behaviour is common to everyone under extreme situations of stress. Thus, one of the most productive ways of increasing flexibility in children with ASDs is to find ways of reducing their stress. Stress in ASD may arise from a number of factors, and to some extent will depend on the individual. Thus, the teacher needs to get to know each individual (and talk to others like parents who know the child well) and the kinds of things that cause that child to be stressed.

Common sources of stress are overstimulation (e.g. from over lit rooms, overcrowded rooms, too much talking), particular phobias (e.g. dogs, leaves), confusion over what to do, where, when, with whom and, most importantly, when it will be over and what will happen then. If the classroom is organised so that there are clear visual answers to all those 'wh'-questions, then this will go a long way to reduce stress and help the child be more responsive to new learning.

Problem solving

Problem: Most of the problems come from not knowing where or how to start and not knowing what to do if a learnt strategy leads to failure or is blocked. The child's attempts to deal with these situations results in refusals to try anything new, anger and frustration when familiar approaches are blocked or unavailable, and catastrophic reactions to failure.

Approach: The principle is to help children with ASDs become more aware of what they know and to provide ways of accessing alternative solutions. Thus the pattern of a set solution to a problem needs to be broken and the child needs to learn several ways to tackle problems. Word processing instead of writing is not only helpful in reducing problems due to clumsiness and consequent poor handwriting, it also eliminates the child's distress at having crosses or crossings out on his or her work, if a mistake is made. Word processing not only enables presentable work at the end but also encourages a process of drafting which is a very good device for teaching flexibility. It demonstrates how drafts are useful parts of the process in learning to tackle a task and that to redraft is not a consequence of getting something wrong, but rather part of the process of getting things right in the end.

Example: Karen was a 12 year old with autism in a small mainstream grammar school in a small town. She was an academically able girl who was generally managing well within the formal structured single sex school. She had always had a problem in accepting any 'mistakes', especially when marked with a cross on her work, but this had only become a significant problem of late when the academic work was becoming harder and parts of essay questions would be judged irrelevant and crossed through with a line. On the return of her homework book on such occasions, Karen would often become very upset and disturbed. She would shout and wail and protest (even when the overall grade she had received was good), sometimes rubbing frantically at the book to try to eliminate the offending line, and sometimes ripping up the book in her anger. She was also beginning to refuse to write essays so she would not get this dreaded line.

She had begun to use a computer both at home and in special lessons at school but it was not the habit of this traditional school to permit word-processed essays. Advocacy from Karen's mother persuaded the school to make an exception for Karen and the immediate problem was solved by the drafting process. However, the school felt that she would be at a disadvantage in examinations unless she also learnt how to use pen and paper for writing essays, and marking was a part of this process. It was thought that now that she was calmer and was using the word processor well to write essays, Karen would accept the return of the old marking system. However, this was not so and, although she continued to write good essays on the word processor, she was as vehement as ever in rejecting the marking of written essays and, moreover, was now reluctant to even write them by hand.

It was decided to introduce a specific and explicit drafting process into the handwriting of essays. Starting with one subject, where the teacher was most cooperative, a homework question was no longer just given out and an essay expected in return. Instead, the first step was for the child to produce a plan for the answer with each point in the plan written on a separate piece of paper. The teacher then went through these pieces of paper with Karen helping her put them in the most effective order to answer the question and removing any that were redundant or irrelevant. It was also sometimes necessary to show Karen where points were missed and a new section heading must be written. The agreed points were then glued in order and Karen took that home to expand into the required essay. Although the essays were not always perfect, it did eliminate gross errors that might formerly have required a line or a cross through them and there was the bonus that Karen had been helped to understand and reflect on the issues of relevance to the question posed. This was such a successful strategy in improving Karen's capacity to write essays, that the teacher decided to introduce a similar process to the class as a whole, to the benefit of all.

Learning to make choices and decisions

Problem: Children with ASDs who attend mainstream schools have usually learnt to make simple choices but it is usually only at the stage of accepting one thing, without any real choice involved. The child may apparently be offered the choice, for example, between pizza or beefburger for lunch but the child can deal with this without making a real choice if he or she just 'chooses' the one thing he or she likes, the pizza say, and ignores the alternative. To be a real choice, the alternatives have to be both held in mind and a choice made between them; it is not just a matter of going along a cafeteria line or a display of activities in the classroom, until something attracts. Unless children with ASDs are given opportunities for making real choices, it is hard for them to understand even when a real choice is there. If they have been taught to conform rather than exercise choice, they may accept things they do not want, simply because they do not know they can refuse both alternatives. In situations of apparent choice, also, the child may avoid choice by always going for the preferred activities (e.g. the computer) and refusing to accept alternatives.

Approach: Children with ASDs need to be given practice in making choices and decisions from an early age. At nursery level, opportunities to make choices for some of the time can, as seen in Chapter 2, help develop a reason for communicating. Thus the High Scope programme (Jordan and Powell 1990) can present a useful framework for getting children to choose the activity they are to do (and to review, or better still reflect on, afterwards) and this kind of approach can be used for free time sessions in later periods of schooling.

In order to make sure the child is making real choices, the cafeteria type situation (whether an actual cafeteria of food or a display of activities on offer as in a classroom set up for a 'choice' of activities) needs to separate the choice making decision from the point of contact with the food or activity items themselves. This can be done by offering a menu at the point of choice and then having that choice 'delivered' by the teacher or monitor. The further and related problem of trying to extend the choices of food or activity that will be contemplated by the child, can be tackled in a similar way. Having a menu enables some control of what is or is not available. If this is very traumatic for the child, menus can be presented at very short intervals so when the first 'course' (whether food or activity) has been selected and consumed, the second menu is offered where the favoured choice once more appears.

Example: Jon, an eight year old in a mainstream primary wanted to be on the computer all the time and found it impossible to 'choose' to do anything else once the computer was available. Even when both computers had been chosen by others who had had their choice before him, he would not choose another activity, but would hover over the person having his or her turn until it was his 'go'. Even when it was not free choice time, he expected to be allowed to do all his work on the computer and had little notion either of sharing with others or taking his turn. He would wait reluctantly, but he would hassle the person having a turn and would not concentrate on anything else as he monitored the situation. He was becoming obsessed with the computer and the teacher was concerned that he was limiting his access to other aspects of the curriculum and to the other skills he needed to acquire.

The principle of not being able to make a choice while dominated by a favourite item, was evident in this scenario. Once the teacher had understood that, she was able to devise a programme for teaching Jon to extend his choices. Choice of activity was moved to a menu board in the cloakroom, but Jon's set pattern of choosing the computer was still evident. However, if it was not his turn for an early choice, and the two computers had been chosen, their pictures were removed from the menu board. Jon then had a forced choice of other items without the visual reminder of the computers. In the classroom, the computers had been resited so they were behind bookcases which screened them from the rest of the class and so Jon was able to complete his 'chosen' activity away from the constant draw of the computer. The teacher also introduced some new exciting activities to compete with the lure of the computers. There was a game with magnets, a circuit board with lights and buzzers, a photography project, cleaning coins with tomato ketchup and similar attractive choices. Eventually, Jon developed wider interests, became less obsessional about time on the computer and gained a greater understanding of what it means to make a choice.

Recalling events

Problem: Children with ASDs seem to have little sense of personal engagement with the events they experience, as if events are being recorded rather than experienced in a conscious way (Powell and Jordan 1997). Thus, when they come to recall those events, they need something that reminds them of the event to cue the response. This is one of the explanations of delayed echoing of phrases that have been acquired or heard in one situation and then seem to 'pop out' when in another situation with some shared feature. It also explains how they can recall whole chunks of text or long lists of things, once a key word is used to trigger the memory of the chunk, and find it easier to tell the teacher what someone else did (someone they have seen and therefore 'recorded') than what they did.

Approach: There are two main areas of attack on this problem. First, the teacher needs to make sure the cues the child can use at the time of learning are made explicit and are ones that can be available to the child at the time of recall. If there are not natural cues with these characteristics, the child needs to be taught memorising strategies which incorporate self-generating cues, such as the use of key imagery or words. The other more fundamental approach is to try to develop the children's sense of themselves performing tasks, and awareness of the knowledge, skills and experiences they are acquiring, at the time of acquisition, and reflection on what is known and what has been experienced.

Example: Nicola was a 13 year old with Asperger's syndrome in a mainstream secondary school. She had spent her first six years of education in a specialist school for children with ASDs, but at secondary level she was moved into the mainstream school into which she had been gradually introduced over the previous year. Academically she seemed very able although she had some limitations in her subject knowledge in certain areas. Nevertheless, the main problems in learning did not seem to lie in her grasp of the subject matter or her ability to do the tasks set, but in her ability to relate her factual knowledge to her experiences and to recall her personal experiences so they could be utilised in literature, drama, history, geography and so on. Teachers would struggle to find the key word that would act as a cue to these apparently inaccessible memories but would find Nicola jumping in with the answer when another child was quizzed, having made no response when she herself was asked the same questions.

A programme was started to encourage Nicola to make her experiences explicit by talking about them at the time and structuring a period of reflection that could later be picked up in recall sessions in other lessons or back in the school, if they were on a trip. At first the process was very strained and artificial with Nicola being prompted to say things like 'It is raining; I am getting wet. The ground is slippery; my feet nearly slipped then' and so on, providing a running commentary on what she was experiencing both in terms of physical events but also impressions and how she was feeling about it. As soon as the experience was over, she would be asked probe questions that matched these commentaries such as 'What was the weather like when we visited the iron bridge? How did you feel walking in the rain?' Then, when asked to write about the visit back at school, the same probe questions could be used, depending on the purpose of the writing.

Here the programme faltered because, although it was increasingly easy to get Nicola to discuss what was happening to her at the time and to answer related questions in a period of reflection immediately after the event, these same questions did not seem sufficient to reliably trigger the memories once back at school, in a totally different situation. On her father's suggestion (the programme had been discussed with the parents and they were following a similar one at home, to increase home–school connections) the teacher tape recorded Nicola's commentary and played that back to her before asking the probe questions back at school. This worked, but it was not clear if Nicola's recall abilities were being improved or if it was just a matter of having found a transportable cue. Nevertheless, the success of this gave Nicola more experience of storing and retrieving personally relevant memories and six months later the taping was faded without much deterioration in performance. However, Nicola still remains dependent on being prompted to make her commentaries and she still needs closely related questions to cue the memories.

Concept development

Problem: Children with ASDs appear to have a poor ability to analyse their experiences and to abstract common patterns from them. This is most apparent in their development of concepts. It is often said that people with ASDs cannot handle abstract concepts, but in fact that is misleading. They can acquire concepts (such as scientific ones) which they construct from their criterial features and they seem to try to use that 'dictionary' way of understanding concepts for all concept acquisition. But everyday concepts such as 'table', 'dog', 'old', 'red' and 'big' are not normally acquired in this way and our 'fuzzy' concepts may not even be able to be defined, even though we have no problem in identifying exemplars of these concepts. We come to understand what these concepts are through our experiences with numerous examples from which we abstract a notion of what constitutes 'tableness', 'dogness', 'oldness', 'redness', 'bigness' and so on. People with autism have problems doing this and end up having to think of particular examples, if they try to think of the concept (Grandin 1995). They may know that other people have a broad concept, say of 'red', but their own thinking seems to be constrained by the particular red of the particular item with which they are associating the concept of red. This has further constraints on the development of conceptual networks and flexible thinking.

Approach: Although there is little scientific evidence of concept development in ASDs, if the experiences that some of them report are true of them all, it is important that teaching concepts should be in ways that help develop more flexible thinking. From early development, labels for everyday objects and their attributes should not be taught by naming particular examples but rather the child should be given lots of experience of sorting by the appropriate category. Only when the child has demonstrated this ability to group many varied examples of the concept in question, should it be labelled. The alternative of teaching that, for example, this brick is 'red' and then having to try to generalise the concept of redness onto red pens, trucks, skirts and different kinds of red will involve as much 'unlearning' as learning and may result in frustration and failure.

Example: Joel was a three year old with autism who was just beginning to develop speech, and attended a mainstream nursery school five mornings a week. His mother had heard about behavioural methods and would often sit him down for 'lessons' in the afternoon to teach him concepts such as his colours and to name common objects from pictures in a book. However, in discussing his programme with the nursery teacher, Joel's mother confided that he seemed to have no idea of what he was doing. He might say 'apple' when shown the picture of one which had been used in the teaching, but he did not use it to name a real apple and certainly not to ask for one. Equally, he could point to the trained item for 'red' but would not then accept other things as being red. Their teaching sessions often ended in mutual frustration, in spite of the rewards she used to keep him 'on task'.

The teacher suggested that she try working on the same concepts as the mother but using the kind of sorting techniques she normally used with the nursery school children. Once she felt Joel had demonstrated understanding of the concept through being able to use it in a variety of structured sorting tasks, she would tell his mother who could then encourage him to use the label to go with that concept in a variety of ways (to label, request, and so on). The pace of the child's learning was slow but it was secure and the mother was much more successful in getting appropriate naming from Joel once he was working on concepts that he understood. The long-term effects on his thinking have yet to be demonstrated, however.

CHAPTER 5

Managing and preventing challenging behaviour

Challenging behaviour and autistic spectrum disorders

Difficult or challenging behaviour is not a part of an autistic spectrum disorder, but it is a common reaction of pupils with these disorders, faced with a confusing world and with very limited abilities to communicate their frustrations or control other people. The corollary of that is that incidents of challenging behaviour tend to reduce as children develop better communication skills, other ways of influencing people and a better understanding of people so that they can make better predictions about what is going to happen. There are times, when a pupil is under particular stress for some reason or when bodily and emotional changes occur at puberty, when behavioural difficulties reoccur and the difference between pupils with an ASD and other pupils is that the former have far fewer ways of defusing their stress and developing coping strategies.

A number of pupils with an ASD will have learning difficulties and/or epilepsy and these conditions are themselves associated with challenging behaviour. Although pupils in mainstream schools are less likely to be suffering from these additional disorders, that will depend in part on educational policies, as explained in Chapter 1. It is also the case that those children who lack speech are more likely to develop severely challenging behaviour, partly because their communication skills are likely to be poorer but also because language is part of the way in which self control can be developed. Thus, young children with autism are more likely to have difficult behaviour pre-school, but the behaviour shown as a toddler is more manageable (the child is smaller) and less unusual when compared to the behaviour of peers. The behavioural outbursts of an older pupil may in reality be less severe, but they appear more frightening because they are more difficult to control, the consequences to the pupil and others are more damaging, and they clearly mark the individual out from peers.

It is also true that more able pupils with an ASD are less likely to display severely challenging behaviour, probably because they are more able to develop some understanding of the world and to have some ways of communicating their needs. Nevertheless, they will share many of the stresses of the less able pupils with an ASD and their greater ability may make their behaviour even more challenging. They may be even more determined to get their own way, to control others, and have the last word or hit. They may take the strategies that adults have devised to

eir behaviour and use them to their own advantage. They may develop
obsessional and narrow interests and be determined to pursue them to
on of all else. Conversely, their greater awareness of their condition may
1 more anxious and even depressed. It is often that group who are at risk
of suicide as they grow up and become aware of their difference from others.

Common problems

Reluctance behaviour

In mainstream classes, however, the day to day management issues in autistic spectrum
disorders are not to do with particular episodes of challenging behaviour but rather
with staff continually having to argue the case with pupils with an ASD. The pupil
might not see why he or she should do something or may be unable to accept that he
or she should submit to the control of the teacher. It is hard for pupils with an ASD to
surrender control to someone they do not understand, cannot predict and, therefore,
cannot trust. Teachers will find it easier to establish control if they offer general and
explicit rules (preferably written and displayed in the classroom) and then encourage
the pupil with an ASD to obey the rule, rather than the teacher. Teachers may even
cheat on occasions by claiming there is a rule in order to get a pupil to do something
(e.g. rather than simply telling a child to go out and play, emphasise that there is a rule
that all the children must go out to play at break times and enlist the pupil's support in
enforcing the rule). If this is over-used, however, there is the danger that the pupil may
learn to turn the tables. This happened to a parent who had tried this management
strategy at home only to find that her son started saying things like, 'There is a rule that
I must stay up until midnight' whenever he wanted something!

It should be noted that the term 'challenging behaviour' is a relative one and one
teacher's 'challenge' may be another's reason for exclusion. It is not always the
severity of the behaviour that leads to the pupil being excluded; it also depends on
the resources (including skill and knowledge) available to the teacher, the stresses
already in the situation, the nature of the school and its overall philosophy.
Challenging behaviour arises out of failure: a failure of the pupil to develop more
productive ways of coping and/or a failure of the school to teach him or her those
ways and to provide a learning environment that meets that pupil's needs. That is
not to allocate blame, but responsibility. A school that is committed to a pupil will
accept the responsibility for teaching that individual to manage without challenging
behaviour. The task is a difficult one and there will be occasional breakdowns, but
regular challenging behaviour in a pupil with an ASD should be a signal that the
school needs to make some further adjustments to meet the pupil's needs.

legal issues too

Running away

Problem: There are two kinds of running behaviour in pupils with an ASD that
present challenges to parents and staff, but only one of them is really running away.
The first kind might more accurately be referred to as 'running to' since it occurs

when the individual has seen some desired object (perhaps miles away from a car or bus) and determinedly escapes from school to run to find it. Since the object of desire is usually connected with a pupil's obsessional interests, and the pupil has usually given away the moment when it was first seen by his or her behaviour at the time, it is usually not too difficult to find the pupil in such a situation. That is not to deny the challenge of such behaviour, since it may have involved a dangerous journey and result in an embarrassing reunion as the pupil is found taking the shiny clothes from the dummy of a window display in a shop, or happily dismantling someone's lawn mower, or sitting in a public fountain.

Yet the more worrying behaviour is the genuine 'running away'. The 'piece of elastic' that normally seems to bind toddlers to their mothers (and that enable forays to explore the world, followed by a swift return) appears to be absent or considerably weakened in ASD. The child will run off without any sign of returning and the panicky adult will then call out to the child to return and start to run after him or her. So begins the training of the child to run away, which is usually started at home and continued by teachers and staff at school to the point where the behaviour has indeed become challenging (i.e. the pursuing adult is no longer able to catch the child). Of course, the adults do not intend to train this behaviour but the child does not respond to intentions, only to his or her own perception of the situation. In this case, there is one game that the child with an ASD always seems to enjoy, even when they do not play any other social games, and that game is chasing. The adult may be anxious or angry, but all that is lost on the child. What he or she perceives is an excited adult making interesting and predictable noises and chasing him or her. Not surprisingly, unless there is an intervention to break this pattern, the behaviour will increase.

Approach: Running away needs to be tackled as early as possible, for the longer the child has been 'trained' to run away, the harder it will be to reverse that training. Nevertheless, even if the child is in his or her teens or is no longer a child, it is still worth trying to prevent this behaviour, if only for the fact that it will interfere with and restrict that person's quality of life. It is better to arrange a block of training, if at all possible, for it will be harder to reverse the original training if the child is still being reinforced for running in other contexts. The principle is to use behavioural methods to train the child to return when his or her name is called. But, as with all attempts to get rid of unwanted behaviour, it must be remembered that the child is enjoying this 'game' and has probably done so for a number of years. Nor does the child have a large range of alternative ways of interacting socially with others. Thus, attempts to eliminate the provoking of chasing (which is how the 'running away' behaviour can be viewed) are unlikely to be entirely successful, unless the child is allowed to engage in chasing at other times. These times need to be clearly signalled, and there should be a different signal for the start of the chasing other than the child running off.

Example: Angela was a six year old with autism in a mainstream primary school, although she had moderate learning difficulties and very limited speech, most of it echolalic. She had been 'running off' since she had been able to run, according to her mother, but it had only seemed challenging in the last year as she began to be able to outpace her mother and teachers were refusing to take her out with the class because she was not safe. There was also the decision to be made of whether she was to stay in the mainstream school or move to a special one. It was felt important to get this behaviour under control before that decision was reached for continued running away would pre-empt a decision in favour of the special school, irrespective of her other needs.

The older and stronger the child is, the more adults will be needed, but the minimum is two. A student teacher volunteered to engage in a programme with the mother every day over the half-term holiday, twice a day. First a suitable reward was chosen. Angela had several obsessional objects she liked to carry around with her and her mother put one of these in her own pocket. A safe environment with a single exit path (a quiet cul de sac) was decided on, and then Angela's mother took her to one end and let her go. She did not call out or run after the child until Angela reached within grabbing distance of the student teacher. At that point, Angela's mother shouted her name in a loud voice and issued the command 'Come here!' At this signal, the student teacher turned Angela round without a word and returned her to her mother. When they reached her, Angela's mother did not tell her off, but praised her for coming back and gave her the toy from her pocket.

This procedure was repeated on fifteen different occasions and then once an evening after school for a further ten occasions, sometimes changing the venue and the reward. The student teacher then arranged to do it in school time with the teacher, first on their own and then with the other children. A session of chasing was introduced into the lunchtime play twice a week but signalled by a bell. A group of children played the game and the lunchtime supervisor rang the bell as the signal for one group of children to run away and a second group to chase them. The programme, then, not only seemed to 'cure' Angela of running away when out, but also led to an integrated social game in the playground at school.

Obsessional objects or activities

Problem: Most, if not all, children with an ASD will develop one or more obsessional interests and/or will have objects to which they are attached and which they insist on carrying everywhere. Sometimes these obsessional behaviours can be challenging in themselves. This may be because they are dangerous, as when, for example, a young boy insisted on walking down the white lines in the middle of the road, regardless of traffic. Or it may be inconvenient to an extreme degree as when a child will only allow the accompanying adult to make turns in one direction (say, only left turns) and becomes consumed with anxiety and then rage if any opposite turns are made. Most commonly in mainstream schools, the obsessional interest becomes challenging when it interferes with the pupil paying attention to anything else and thus prevents any new learning.

Approach: As with all challenging behaviour, the first step is to find out what function the behaviour is serving for the pupil. An obsessional act may be a way of reducing or managing anxiety, or it may block out other confusing stimuli, or it may be a source of pleasure and all consuming interest because it provides order and security in a confusing world. In nearly all cases, one of the key functions is to give the pupil a sense of being in control. Once the particular functions have been discovered, the teacher must realise that those functions will need to be replaced (or the need for them removed) if there is to be any chance of getting the pupil to diminish or give up the obsessional activity. If this is not done, even if a programme does remove one particular unwanted behaviour, it may come back or a new and even worse behaviour may take its place. All behaviour has a purpose, even if that purpose is not immediately apparent to us, and we need to teach a new way of fulfilling that purpose if the programme is to succeed.

Example: Mathew was an 11 year old with autism in a middle school. He had had many different obsessions, with new ones usually taking the place of the old, but occasionally with two or more co-existing but at different strengths. None of the obsessional interests were of themselves severely challenging but, as Mathew got older, they increasingly interfered with his studies and were currently a threat to his remaining in mainstream. At the time of the intervention, Mathew had an obsessional interest in churches.

The church interest seemed like a good candidate for the principle that obsessional interests are best broadened out, rather than suppressed. It did not seem to serve a function of anxiety reduction but rather it gave Mathew pleasure to look at the architecture of churches and to make lists of the location of churches he had visited and all kinds of statistics about their construction. The first tack then, was to incorporate the study of churches into most of the subjects in the curriculum that he was required to study. Some of this worked fairly well; he drew stained glass in art lessons, listened to church music, wrote essays about his visits to churches, studied the history of a particular church and looked at how churches were constructed and where they were located for science and geography, respectively. But these studies did not always fit what his peers were doing, nor did it work in extending his interest from the churches themselves to the subjects in which they were embedded. In fact, all these opportunities to study churches just seemed to feed and increase his interest. The one success of the programme so far was that it had rid the classroom of conflict between Mathew and his teachers and had made Mathew keen to do his work.

It was decided to continue with the church interest in lessons where it was appropriate (e.g. in personal writing, some art and music lessons) but to insist on some non-church related work in some lessons first, before he was allowed to pursue his interest. He was given an amount of work to get through, rather than a time period, or he would have wasted that time arguing and protesting about having to do the work and then only attempting it half-heartedly. To begin with, he only had a very short non-church task to perform before being allowed to indulge in his church 'work', but this was lengthened gradually until it occupied the bulk of the lesson, with the church study being a 'filler' once his main work was over. The programme was successful and the interest in churches became less obsessional and more like a special hobby.

This second approach is a good one for coping with the change in obsessional interest. In Mathew's case, he developed a new obsessional interest in alarm systems towards the end of the programme. It may be that the programme contributed to his change of interest, except that this commonly occurs, and he had changed interests before. If the programme had remained the first one of utilising his interest and broadening it out into all his curriculum subjects, the change in obsessional interest would have meant an enormous extra burden on the teacher to change all the curriculum materials once more to take account of the new interest. Nor is there any guarantee of how long an interest will last and alarm systems are not as conducive to curriculum enrichment as churches!

On balance, then, the second approach appears the more appropriate choice for the mainstream teacher, but there are two points to make. The first is that using the pupil's interest is a great motivator for the pupil. During the first programme Mathew was really enthused with his work and learnt new skills at a rate he never achieved in the second programme. The second point is that the reward programme may not have worked if it had been introduced first, at a time when Mathew was not interested in doing anything else other than study his churches. The first programme gave him a chance to find some interest in the curriculum and to develop good work habits. There is never any single solution to a problem and the choice for each pupil in each situation may be somewhat different.

Aggression

Problem: Aggression is not really an appropriate description for what is seen in individuals with an ASD, although that is what the behaviour may appear to be. It depends on whose viewpoint is considered. One can witness an incident where a pupil with an ASD appears to lash out viciously at other pupils or at staff, with no discernible provocation and in a way that the injured parties would certainly perceive as 'aggressive'. Yet, if we discuss such incidents with the people with the ASD who are able to discuss their feelings, they do not report any feelings of anger towards their victims nor any desire to inflict harm on them. Most commonly they describe themselves as being in a panic and with little awareness of what they have done. In other words, most apparent acts of aggression are reactions to events that have panicked the individual and not a conscious assault on another person. That does not mean that the behaviours themselves should be tolerated, nor that the pupil with the ASD should not be taught to take responsibility for his or her actions. But it does mean that there is little point in straight punishment or sanctions. Using any form of aversives is likely to backfire because it will increase the pupil's confusion and panic and is then more likely to increase the 'aggressive' behaviour.

Approach: Once again, the approach should be to determine the function of the behaviour, as well as any particular trigger in that situation. Given the extreme levels of stress experienced by many pupils with an ASD, from just existing in a social world like school, there may be no particular trigger in the sense that that trigger has 'caused' the behaviour. What is more likely is that the trigger is the last straw for the pupil who has undergone a series of stressful events, and that in less stressful circumstances the aggressive act would not have been triggered. The situation should be studied with that knowledge in mind, plus individual knowledge of the pupil and the things that are likely to lead to stress.

A further analysis should view the behaviour as a form of communication (whether or not this was the pupil's underlying intention) and to ask what it is that the pupil would be trying to communicate in this situation, if the pupil knew how to communicate. Treating the behaviour as communication, and attempting to substitute a better form of communication that will serve the same function, may be the most helpful way of dealing with this kind of behaviour. Finally, the pupil may need teaching to make him or her aware of what they have done and the points at which they had choices which could have led to alternative behaviour. They need to understand that sanctions are a direct result of their own behaviour (for which they must accept responsibility) and not simply the result of getting caught and therefore the fault of the person who has enforced the rule. A flow chart showing the relationships between actions and events and showing choice points can be helpful in bringing these points home to the pupil.

Example: Luke was a ten year old with Asperger's syndrome in a mainstream primary school who was in danger of being excluded because of a succession of 'aggressive' acts against teachers, support staff and other pupils. There appeared to be no common thread to these incidents in terms of any immediate cause, except that they all resulted in someone being hit, kicked, or bitten without apparent provocation. Luke's parents also reported similar incidents at home and a psychologist from the local behavioural support team was involved in developing a strategy to try to deal with the situation.

Luke had good structural language but could offer little insight into his own behaviour. It was apparent that in each case he was very upset at the time but he could not say why he had directed his 'aggressive' act to the person involved nor what they had done to upset him. Talking to the other people involved, or those who had witnessed incidents, and observing some later incidents that occurred, the psychologist suggested the following range of functions for these acts.

In the classroom, when there was a lot of noise and confusion and the task he was engaged in required concentration, Luke became increasingly stressed. A pupil jogged his arm unintentionally and Luke reacted almost automatically by biting the pupil's arm, which was in line with his mouth at the time. This seemed such an automatic act that there would be little chance of getting Luke to learn to inhibit his action in such a situation. Thus a better approach, was to try to reduce the confusion in the classroom by giving Luke a secure and single place to work, especially for tasks that required concentration.

In the playground, Luke seemed once more bewildered by all the activity and spent his time going round the perimeter fence, occasionally stopping to watch the others fearfully, often flinching and putting his hands over his ears. When a pupil, engaged in another game and oblivious of Luke, came charging towards him, Luke 'defended' himself with a pre-emptive hit to the girl's head. The motivation this time seemed to be fear and defensiveness rather than frustration, but the action seemed equally removed from Luke's conscious control. The approach chosen was to reduce the amount of time Luke had to spend in the playground and when there, he was taught how to play simple games with a small group of buddies who protected him from the general hubbub and confusion. Meantime a classroom programme helped Luke learn the difference between intentional and accidental behaviour, although this was a very difficult concept for him to grasp.

Finally, a teaching incident was analysed. Luke had been told that he just had to do a particular worksheet of mathematical problems and then he could go back to the Lego model he was intent on building. But, because he completed the worksheet so quickly, the teacher gave him another one to do (possibly forgetting what she had said, or not realising the importance it would have for Luke). He bit her. Clearly this is not an acceptable reaction on Luke's part, but it is an understandable one. The importance of keeping to agreed rules and contracts was emphasised, but Luke was also given explicit instruction about how to be assertive about what he considered a breach of fairness, rather than resorting to violence. This needed role play and lots of prompting in real situations, but there were instances of him using this strategy.

Overall, the strategies for the different situations were effective in reducing Luke's 'aggressive' behaviour. This piecemeal approach does not ensure that he may not resort to violence in new situations, but it is usually more effective than trying to apply a blanket strategy to all incidents, regardless of cause or function. Above all, it is important to deal with each function before secondary functions emerge. Very often a pupil may start doing something for one reason (e.g. biting, out of a sense of frustration) but will then begin to use the same action for other functions (e.g. out of boredom, or to effect predictability). Once that has happened, it becomes far more difficult to get the pupil's behaviour under control.

CHAPTER 6

Working with parents and carers

Note: In this chapter the term 'parent' is used as shorthand for anyone who has a parental role.

What do parents have to offer staff?

First and foremost, parents have detailed and excellent knowledge over time about their own child, much of which can be extremely useful for those who are working in school. Autism affects many, if not all, aspects of children's lives including their communication, self-help skills, their academic performance and their social interactions with peers, their family and with adults. Pupils with an ASD have a different way of viewing and responding to the world and in learning and developing skills. They also differ from each other in terms of their abilities, their personality and the extent to which their autism affects them. It is therefore necessary for staff to have general knowledge of autism and particular information about the pupil. The parents are in an excellent position to supply these specific details about their child.

It is important to meet the pupil's parents and to keep in regular contact with them. Without this, both staff and parents might speculate about what happens at home or school (often on the basis of the pupil's behaviour) and such speculation and guesswork can be inaccurate and unhelpful. The time, venue and frequency of meetings will need to be negotiated with parents. Parents should have the opportunity to speak to those in most frequent contact with the pupil such as the class teacher, head of year and support assistant and those people may need to be freed of teaching commitments to enable this to happen in school time.

Suggestion: Ask the parents the following questions, as a minimum:

- What type of activities does your child enjoy?
- What does your child appear to dislike or to find upsetting?
- How does your child communicate with you at home?
- What is the best way of helping your child to understand what you want?
- How is it best to calm your child when he or she is upset?
- What have you used as incentives to encourage him or her to do something you want?

In addition, many parents will have done a great deal of reading about autism or Asperger's syndrome and therefore have much useful information they could pass on to staff. They may have video material or booklets which they would be happy to share.

Suggestion: Ask the parents whether they have any information on autism or Asperger's syndrome which they could show you.

How do the parents feel?

Clearly, it is not possible to know how a parent is actually feeling, as we all react differently. The feelings of parents of children with an ASD will differ depending on the nature of their past experiences with schools, their relationships with other professionals, the other demands they have on their time and the resources to address these, and the degree to which they and others find their child's behaviour distressing or challenging. The range of emotions they are likely to have felt include feelings of failure, anger, sadness, loss, guilt, frustration, isolation, inadequacy embarrassment and hopelessness, in addition to positive feelings of love, happiness, pride, and satisfaction when their child has shown success or they have felt a sense of achievement in something they have done for the child. It is likely that the feelings and anxieties most parents have about their children's education will be heightened for parents of pupils with an ASD.

Most parents of children with an ASD will have spent many hours thinking about which school and which approaches are likely to be of most benefit to their child and are likely to go on thinking about this throughout their child's education. They will need much reassurance that the school placement is working well and be anxious if feedback from staff suggests otherwise. Their current feelings with the situation and their past experiences need to be borne in mind by staff. How staff respond to them and vice versa will determine how the interaction proceeds. Just as we have stressed that it is important to be empathic and to 'get into the pupil's shoes', it is also important to 'get into the parents' shoes'.

Suggestion: A useful triad of questions.

Triad of Questions
(where 'X' could be a classroom activity/a problem behaviour/
home–school contact/homework)

- How do the parents see X?
- What can we do/have we done to enable the parents to understand X?
- Have the parents the opportunity (and the means) to give their views on X?

'Circle friends' and groups for parents

In earlier chapters, mention was made of circle of friends work. Parents often report that their pupil has little or no contact with children outside the family – and that their own contact with friends and family may be quite restricted. By forming a circle of friends for the pupil, you may also form a network of support for the parents. It is important to consider whether the parents would value meeting other parents and whether there are existing groups to which you might introduce the parents (e.g. local autistic society; parent–teacher group; parent group at a neighbouring school). Some parents might prefer to meet other families on an individual basis and this could be explored by asking the parents about their contact with other parents of children with an ASD and whether they would like to explore or expand such contact.

The needs of other family members

There may be other family members who have contact with the school either currently or in the future. The pupil may have brothers or sisters who attend the school and grandparents or other relatives who collect the pupil from school or attend reviews. It is important to seek the views of parents on the extent to which the brothers and sisters of the pupil with autism might be involved. Some parents are happy for their other children to play a supporting role and see that as a benefit of the placement. Other parents feel that it is important for them not to have responsibilities within school for their brother or sister. It is important that other adults who play a significant part in the child's life are given an opportunity to contribute their views. They could be invited to reviews, write in the home–school book or attend open sessions for parents. The pupil's parents should be asked if there are other adults who play such a role and whether they would like them to be involved in any way in school.

Working with parents

Responding to offers from parents

Parents may volunteer to contribute in some way, which may include supporting their child or others in the same class, working in other parts of the school, or talking to the staff about autism. Staff need to consider how to respond to such requests – in particular the implications for the pupil and others within the school. Ideally, there would be a whole-school policy on how parents might be involved and this would guide the discussions.

Responding to requests from parents

There are many different approaches to autism and the parents might want staff to follow a particular approach at school. Some approaches or elements of these might fit well into usual school practice, but others might demand that staff work in a very different way which might be difficult logistically because of the staffing or resources needed or run counter to the school's philosophy and rationale. It is important to listen carefully to requests and suggestions, irrespective of any initial reactions or personal views and to discuss the implications for the pupil and others of following the approach within school.

Involving and informing parents

It is important that parents are offered a similar range of options by the teachers they meet as the pupil moves through the school and that this is within the framework of the whole-school policy on how parents are involved and informed. Not all parents value the same things in terms of home–school partnership. Some parents want to be actively involved with work at the school and other parents want to be informed of their pupil's progress but are not able to, or do not wish to, work directly with staff or the pupil in school. Particularly useful areas where school staff can work together with parents, and have an impact, are in sharing their ideas on developing communication, creating a social group for the pupil, behaviour management strategies and in deciding on priorities and future placement.

Home–school book

Many schools use a home–school book for the pupil in which both the parents and the school staff can give information of interest and value to the other. This might include written reports, extracts of the pupil's work and photographs and a summary of what the pupil did during the school day or in the evening or the weekend. It is important that the book contains material from staff and parents which is of sufficient detail to be useful and which is positive in tone – even where incidents of problem behaviour might be reported. For example, rather than simply writing, 'Ben had a bad day today' – to give information on which parts of the day were difficult and some examples of incidents which led to his day being described as 'bad'. Staff can also try to extract something positive from this by continuing with something along the lines of 'so we have decided to do X next time' or by asking for the parents' views on what they feel might help.

Showing parents how the pupil spends the day

Many parents of pupils with an ASD would love to know more about how their child spends his or her day. Pupils are often unable or unwilling to tell their parents much about this themselves. While parents of normally developing children often also complain that their child does not say much about school, at least most parents have an idea of what happens in ordinary schools – but they do not know so much about what happens when a pupil has different needs. How are these met? How does the pupil manage with the various sessions and activities during the day? It is possible in some cases for the parents to observe the pupil directly within school, but where this might affect the pupil and others, then other methods need to be used. Some schools take a video of the pupil in different situations and use this at review meetings with parents. Parents should be asked if they would like to see how their child works and plays at school and consulted on how this might be arranged.

Homework

Work set by staff at school for the pupil to complete at home can cause difficulties for the pupil and his or her parents. Pupils may be reluctant to do the work as they see school as the place for school work or they may fail to write down or understand the task or strive for hours to produce a perfect product. Often the pupil with an ASD is able to read complex sentences without understanding or extracting the meaning and this can lead staff to overestimate their ability and set tasks which are too demanding. In addition, some pupils with an ASD can have the factual knowledge required but fail to recall this unless they receive particular prompts, or they may be reluctant to record what they know on paper. Some may have dyspraxia or specific learning difficulties in addition to their ASD which makes written work very difficult. Again, their ability to talk with ease about a topic might cause staff to think the pupil has been lazy when they come to mark the pupil's limited or poorly presented written work. This can cause stress for the parents and lead to difficulties for the pupil when they produce their homework. Discussions about what is sensible in terms of homework, including alternative means of presentation such as word processing or dictation, or completing work at school, are vital, to avoid extra pressures on the pupil and others.

Reviews of the pupil

The majority of pupils with an ASD will be identified at one of the assessment stages 2 to 5 of the Code of Practice (DfE 1994). As such, they will have an Individual Education Plan which should be reviewed with the parents on a regular basis. There should be space on the Plan for the parents' contributions and they should be invited to suggest and agree possible target areas and to be involved in working on these, if they wish. Where the pupil is considered able to contribute to the review, then this should be arranged in a way that is appropriate to the pupil. The objectives for IEPs should include developing an understanding of self and others, teaching for independence and developing communication skills. There should not be too much of a focus on what the pupil can not do with a result that much teaching and time is spent on tasks he or she finds difficult, but a focus on how staff are to enable the pupil to work towards targets that are of value and relevance in a way that is interesting and enjoyable for the pupil.

For a secondary-aged pupil, it will be useful to identify the subjects in which particular targets might be addressed. Reviews of IEPs provide an extremely useful opportunity for staff–parent discussions on the pupil's progress and areas of strength and for parents and staff to raise concerns or areas which each might be able to work on with the pupil. Ideally, prior to the review of the IEP, parents should be sent a written report on the pupil's progress and invited to consider their views of the pupil and the areas on which they might like the school to work. After the review meeting, they should be given a copy of the IEP. Some parents may want to contribute their views in writing prior to the meeting, so that participants will be able to give these thought before the review.

Other parents at the school

With the increasing attention being given to the inclusion of pupils with more complex and demanding special educational needs, there is a need to address the concerns of staff and other parents about the potentially detrimental effect and the positive outcomes of this policy on the education and well-being of other pupils. The views of parents of other pupils at the school can influence the success of the placement and it is important to consider how they are informed and how issues are addressed when raised. There are likely to be other parents at the school whose pupils also have SEN and it may be useful to set up a group for these parents and/or with parents of normally developing pupils to discuss issues of inclusion which they then feedback to the larger staff and parent groups. Even where it is not possible to have a room within the school wholly designated for parents' use, having a space which is regularly timetabled for parents is likely to encourage parent activity and signals that they are welcome in the school.

The pupil's behaviour at home and school

When life at school and home is going well for the pupil, and parents and staff are receiving positive reports from each other, it is likely that parent–staff relationships will be easy to develop and maintain. However, both staff and parents need to prepare for times when the child's behaviour or performance might be viewed as a problem either at home or at school. Staff–parent relationships might then be more difficult. It is possible, for example, for each to blame the other for something they are doing or not doing with the pupil. It is important in these instances to gather information on the nature of the problem and on the factors which might be contributing to this at home and school. It can be easy to take the quick route and guess what the cause might be, without making adequate enquiries and getting clear, factual information from all involved. Engaging in speculation is not helpful and is likely to lead to the apportioning of blame and ineffective solutions. This is particularly true when the child's behaviour appears to be very different at home from his or her behaviour at school. Pupils may pose no major behaviour problems to staff and be very undemanding and well behaved in school. When they arrive home, however, they may engage in challenging behaviour towards their brothers, sisters or their parents. It seems as if the pupil manages to contain all the anxieties and difficulties experienced at school and releases these on returning home.

For some children, the reverse scenario is true, particularly when the child first starts attending school. The child may be relatively easy to manage at home, perhaps because the environment is fairly constant and familiar and there are few demands to be sociable or to engage in tasks which are not interesting to them. In school, they find themselves in what is to them a noisy, confusing, social environment where people attempt to communicate with them in ways which they often do not understand. In addition, they are encouraged to engage in tasks which may hold little interest or meaning for them. Their reaction is to try to sabotage the activity or to escape or to do nothing, all of which challenge the teaching staff. When parents and staff hear very different accounts about the same child, they may find it hard to believe or they can be quick to blame the other. It is important to acknowledge that very different behaviour at home and school is a phenomenon found in some children with an ASD (as it can be in others).

In general, there is a need for consistency of approach between classrooms, between adults and between parents and staff. Some authors have even written about the need for a 24 hour curriculum for a child with an ASD (Jordan and Powell 1995b). In essence, this means that it is important not just to consider what occurs within the school day, but also to give thought to the pupil's total waking hours. Where parents and staff can share strategies and adopt a similar approach to communication and behaviour management, for example, this is likely to be in the interests of the child. Both staff and parents may feel that they have useful strategies to share and would like the other to try this at home or school. They can feel let down and disappointed if the other party does not take up the idea or use the strategy they have suggested. However, it is important for staff to realise that not all parents, even those who have the time, want to adopt a teacher stance in relation to their child. So suggestions from staff that the parents introduce a particular communication system at home or work on homework with the child may not be taken up. Similarly, ideas which parents have might be difficult for staff to implement in the face of other demands upon the teacher. So, any discussions about the sharing of strategies between home and school need to involve discussion of the logistics and the personal feelings of those involved.

An example of effective staff–parent partnership

There are some mainstream schools where staff have developed very effective and successful ways of working with parents of children with special educational needs, including those with an ASD. Other mainstream schools have not had the experience of having children who are very different and who require changes to be made to the way in which staff organise and work with pupils. They have not had to give serious thought to how parents of these children might feel and to the demands parents might make. Nor have they often been given much advice and support from visiting professionals on how to do this. Sadly, in these cases, the relationships between staff and parents deteriorate and the child may have to move school as a result. This is demonstrated by the following case study of a family and their experience of two mainstream schools.

Example: Billy is an able seven year old child with Asperger's syndrome who has developed speech and language which he can use to communicate with others. He is described by his parents as a clumsy child who has difficulty organising himself and who finds drawing and writing activities difficult. Billy was formally assessed by the LEA when at nursery school and it was recommended that he should attend a mainstream school with 20 hours additional support when he reached the age of five years. His parents visited mainstream schools in their local area and chose a school which seemed happy to accept him. A support assistant was appointed who developed a good relationship with Billy.

At his first review, however, Billy's mother was concerned about some of the comments made. The staff seemed to be expecting Billy to behave like the other five year olds in his group. One target staff had set was that 'Billy should learn to make friends with sensible children'. His mother felt the staff knew little about autistic spectrum disorders and so they could not be blamed for these expectations. She therefore provided the staff with as much information as she could. She was not given a copy of his IEP and asked later for this. She had to ask several times. When she became more assertive in her requests, the head teacher said, 'I don't know why you are so concerned about the IEP, it's only a piece of paper.' His mother also asked to have a meeting with the SENCO to discuss Billy's progress, but this was not arranged as she was told the SENCO had a full teaching timetable.

Billy's mother was prepared to continue working with the school as she felt sure Billy would benefit from being with ordinary children and she did not want to introduce a change of school in case this distressed him. However, after almost two terms at the school, she finally decided to take action when Billy started to cry on Sunday evenings, saying that he did not want to go to school. She decided to look for another mainstream school, but she had lost her confidence in choosing a school as she thought she had chosen the right one in the first place. She was afraid about the effects on Billy if she chose another school that did not work well. However, she did have more of an idea of what she might look for, i.e. willingness of staff to meet with her and share the IEP, and evidence that they would change things to meet Billy's needs.

She arranged visits to two mainstream schools and fairly quickly decided which of the two schools to choose. The staff were very welcoming to her from the start and said that they had had experience of an older boy with an ASD. They said that they were very positive about inclusion and would not easily be disturbed by challenging behaviour. The head teacher said that she would invite Billy's mother to the interview to appoint the support assistant – not that she would have the main say – but acknowledging that her view would be important. The staff showed her work done by the pupil with an ASD which had detailed notes from staff on how he had completed the task and the type of help he had needed. In addition, they said that at playtimes, their policy was to teach all the children how to play effectively with each other and that Billy would be part of this.

Billy has now been at the school for a year and the promises and offers made on the first visit have all been fulfilled. Billy's mother attended the interview for the assistant. The assistant has been funded to attend a two-term course on ASD and she has developed a very good relationship with Billy. Billy has told his parents that he loves his new school and is noticeably happier. His parents feel that the staff have the confidence and skills to respond positively to their requests and to solve any problems that might arise for Billy.

Both schools were in the same LEA, yet the attitudes and practice were very different, with serious consequences for the child and his family. Some of the ideas and suggestions given in this chapter may help to enhance the situation in mainstream schools for other children and their families so that the experience of all concerned is positive rather than negative.

CHAPTER 7

Working collaboratively – whole-school practice

People involved in the school life of a pupil with an autistic spectrum disorder

Schools are complex systems and it is important to consider how the many adults a pupil is likely to meet work together to provide a consistent environment which reflects the pupil's particular needs and is conducive to their well-being. Table 7.1 shows the number of people who might impinge on the life of a pupil with an ASD in the classroom, the school and beyond.

Each of these groups is likely to need and to acquire different types and amounts of information. This raises questions of who needs to know what and why and who should decide on this. Clearly, the parents, the class teacher and the pupil are the people who should have the main say. Teachers need to consider what information, at a minimum, other people need to know about the pupil.

Table 7.1: People involved with a pupil with an ASD

Within the pupil's class	Pupil
	Pupil's family
	Class teacher/Form teacher
	Support assistant
	Classmates
Within the school	Head teacher
	SENCO
	Other teachers
	Other pupils
	Other classroom staff
	Other parents
	Lunchtime supervisors
	Clerical staff
	Caretaker
	Drivers and escorts
Visitors	Visiting professionals
	Other visitors
	Volunteers
	School Governors

It would be useful to explain:

- that the pupil will have difficulties in communication and may not understand what is said to him or her, even though his or her own speech and language might be quite good;
- how others can make themselves understood to the pupil;
- that the pupil may say and do things which appear to be personally insulting, that they may lack the usual inhibitions and tend to say what he or she sees and feels, with little idea of the impact on the people around;
- ways of interacting with the pupil that are not anxiety-provoking;
- how to respond when the pupil behaves inappropriately.

Shared understandings between staff

Good communication systems between staff within a school are essential for the welfare of all pupils and not just for those with an ASD. Pupils with an ASD are likely to be more vulnerable to gaps or flaws in the school's communication system than others. Poor communication is likely to lead to inconsistency and inappropriate action by staff and pupils. Staff need to understand the nature of the specific needs of a pupil with an ASD and the rationale for the strategies used, so that they interact with and manage the pupil effectively and support rather than undermine their colleagues' work. Without this understanding, the pupil's behaviour may be viewed as naughty and a teacher's responses 'soft' or 'unfair'. Staff have to decide together in which areas of school life the pupil might need to be treated differently from others and that priorities for the pupil with an ASD might be different from those of pupils of the same age. It may help to generate a list of do's and don'ts for adults in a supervisory role when they first start working with a pupil. Positive reports on the pupil from others are likely to be conducive to success.

Knowing a pupil has an ASD and receiving general information on autism directs staff to the way in which such pupils view the world and how they think and learn, but does not give information on how each individual pupil will react or behave within their school. So in addition to this background knowledge, the staff need information on the needs of the particular pupil or pupils with ASD who attend their school. Much useful information can be obtained from the pupil's parents (see Chapter 6).

At a minimum, the pupil's class teacher or subject teacher(s) and support assistant (if allocated) should be given information on ASD and its implications for the pupil. However, it would also be valuable if other staff who may meet the pupil receive information. Within the school's special needs policy document, it would be helpful to have a section on the specific needs of pupils with an ASD. In addition, the School Governors, who may need to advise on matters raised by staff or parents in connection with the pupil, should be given this information.

Information for staff might be in written form – a basic outline of ASD and then information on the particular characteristics of each pupil, what the pupil enjoys or dislikes and how he or she communicates. If in-service sessions on ASD are arranged, then it is helpful to invite as many adults in contact with the pupil, as possible. It may be helpful to generate a set of rules for staff to use in relation to the pupil in order to manage particular situations consistently (e.g. repetitive questioning; greetings; dress; inappropriate behaviour).

The need for a named staff member

Within the school, it is important that a member of staff, with whom the pupil has frequent contact, is identified as having a particular responsibility for that pupil. In a primary school, this is likely to be the pupil's class teacher. In a secondary school, this could be the pupil's registration teacher or the head of year. This teacher would develop an understanding and relationship with the pupil and act as an advocate. They would also be responsible for collating and facilitating the information exchange between members of staff and relevant others. They should not, however, be seen as the person with sole responsibility for the pupil – responsibility and care should be shared. As the pupil's ability to understand and negotiate develops, he or she should be consulted and closely involved in the decisions made and actions taken. In the past, much of what has been arranged for individuals with an ASD has been done without asking their opinion. Things have been done *to* them rather than *with* them. Interventions introduced in this way, without discussion, are likely to fail and may be unethical.

The role of the support assistant

Some pupils with an ASD may be allocated support from an adult who may work within the classroom or elsewhere. They may be qualified nursery nurses or have child care qualifications or may not have any relevant qualifications at all. Some are appointed by the school staff and others are allocated to the school by the local authority. Much thought and discussion should occur to determine how and when the support assistant should work with the pupil. It is possible to envisage a scenario where the support assistant is almost always the person who supports the pupil in an activity and other people in the classroom (i.e. the class teacher and the other pupils) may be unwittingly excluded. It is possible too for the support assistant to be the pupil's only friend. This then limits the knowledge and understanding of the pupil that others develop and, equally important, it can feel very burdensome for the support assistant. The knowledge and understanding about the pupil with an ASD should be shared throughout the classroom and beyond and not remain solely with the support assistant.

Shared understandings amongst the pupils

One of the potential strengths of attendance at a mainstream school for a pupil with an ASD is the opportunity for the pupil to work with others who are developing normally. Schools with effective policies and practice on promoting cooperation and positive peer relationships will be conducive to the placement of a pupil with an ASD. Other pupils will know that the pupil is different, as their own attempts to relate to them will be affected. Discussions to determine what information other pupils are given about his or her needs, and whether this is limited to the pupil's class or goes beyond, would be valuable. The pupil's parents should be consulted for their views on this. Creating a circle of friends (Taylor 1997, Whitaker *et al.* 1998) would provide practical and emotional support for the pupil during work and leisure activities within and outside school (see Chapter 3 on social understanding). There are potentially important gains for other pupils at the school in learning to understand and accommodate the different ways in which pupils with an ASD perceive the world. Initially, these pupils may need support from staff to relate successfully to the pupil, but with time, support from peers may occur naturally with minimum input.

Managing aspects of the school day

Pupils with an ASD often find it difficult to know what they are supposed to do when they are with other pupils and staff they do not know and where the activities may be unfamiliar. Whenever they are confused, it is likely that they will behave inappropriately. It may be helpful to indicate where they should sit or stand by using a mat or to allow them to take something of interest to them into the session. Other staff and pupils may need an explanation for this strategy. Once the pupil with an ASD has learned a routine or a set of rules for a particular activity or situation at home or school (e.g. bedtime; route to school; place in classroom), they can be very upset when a change is made to this – as they then cannot easily predict what might happen next. So, if a change has to be made to a familiar routine or situation, the pupil should be prepared for this in advance, if possible. However, some changes are so anxiety-producing that it may be better not to allow a prolonged period of anticipation; this will need to be discussed with the parents.

Transitions from one class to the next

As pupils with an ASD find it hard to work out the rules for particular sessions, they can find difficulty in moving from one situation (where they have become certain about what they are doing) to another. Within a school day, there are many such changes and these increase for pupils in secondary education. It is important to make it visually clear to the child what happens and where. Making their way to different parts of the school might be difficult for a number of reasons which need to be analysed and appropriate strategies devised. Classmates could accompany the pupil or the pupil could be given a map or photographs of where to go next. The movement and noise of many pupils moving simultaneously can be frightening and anxiety-provoking and it may be valuable to allow the pupil to leave the classroom slightly earlier or later with another pupil or pupils perhaps from his or her circle of friends group.

When the pupil has to change teacher or classroom, it is important that he or she is prepared for this change. In a secondary school, this happens several times a day and a pupil may need to be prepared towards the end of each lesson to pack up their equipment and to be reminded where they are going next. A visual timetable would help. For primary pupils, a change of classroom usually occurs only once a year and then visits can be made to the new classroom and teaching time spent with the new class teacher. The pupil could be accompanied by another pupil and/or a supporting adult. This might be supplemented by the use of photographs of the new classroom – possibly with a photograph of the pupil sitting in his or her new place. It is helpful to the pupil if the general rules for behaviour and classroom procedure apply across all classes. If particular strategies have been used successfully with the pupil in one classroom, information on these should be passed to the other staff and the strategies continued if still necessary and appropriate. If this is not possible, it will be important to explain carefully to the pupil how the rules may be different in a particular class and why this is so.

Transitions between people

A pupil with an ASD will potentially meet several adults and pupils during the course of a school day. Pupils with an ASD have difficulty in reading the thoughts and intentions of other people and so may act in a way which seems defiant, unacceptable or inappropriate. Their own facial expression might not match their current emotion, so they may fail to look confused or upset. Without an understanding of autism and the pupil's particular abilities and difficulties, adults may view the pupil as naughty, rude or emotionally disturbed. So, all adults who may meet the pupil require some basic information on ASD and the pupil.

In addition, the following key principles might be usefully adopted by adults to guide the nature of their interactions:

- approach the pupil in a way that does not surprise or shock the pupil;
- keep at a comfortable distance from the pupil;
- use a quiet tone of voice;
- have a purpose to the interaction – other than purely social;
- continue with the interaction whether or not the pupil is looking at them;
- use a form of communication that the pupil understands;
- assess whether the pupil is likely to be able to understand and respond to the request;
- give the pupil time to respond;

- teach them to say when they need help or do not understand;
- create a balance between tasks they find difficult and those which they can do more easily.

The personal style of teachers and adults will vary and we would not suggest that all adults within the school, or in contact with the pupil, should try to be identical; but they should give careful thought as to how they interact with the pupil.

'High risk' times or areas

A useful exercise is to identify within a typical school day and week, the times, sessions and activities that work well for the pupil and staff and those which are cause for concern. It is then useful to identify the features of the positive and less positive times and consider whether you can introduce the features linked to positive times to other parts of the day. Or you may want to consider expanding the time spent on positive activities and reduce the time spent on those which cause concern, whilst keeping a broad and relevant curriculum.

As autism affects many aspects of the pupil's development and functioning, it is important to consider situations outside the classroom as well as what occurs within it – in particular at lunchtimes and break times. Pupils with an ASD usually find unstructured times where pupils are 'free to choose' what they do and with whom, very difficult, as each time the rules they are trying to elicit seem to change. Many spend the time alone engaging in repetitive activities or routines or attempt to interact with other pupils but fail to sustain such interaction. They therefore require support from adults or other pupils, as described earlier in the circle of friends work, to develop their social understanding and to protect them from being teased by others. Providing apparatus, materials or an activity at break times, or shortening the time they spend outside the building, can be helpful.

Establishing links with agencies outside the school

Within the local authority area, there will be other sources of information and support including other mainstream and special schools and units which have pupils with an ASD on roll and professionals who have a particular interest or responsibility for pupils with an ASD. An increasing number of authorities also have an outreach teacher or team to support staff teaching pupils with an ASD in mainstream schools. There may be a local autistic society which can supply information on local support groups, interested personnel and resources. It is useful to identify these sources and to ask about the nature of their work and resources for such pupils and their families.

Questions concerning the most appropriate placement

When staff and the pupil experience major difficulties over an extended period of time, it is likely that questions may be raised about whether the placement is in the best interests of the pupil. Suggestions of other types of placement or provision might be offered by staff who teach the child, other staff who do not, but observe the child, or the child's parents or other parents of children at the school. These questions can be discussed at the pupil's review, but if a review is not planned for some time, an additional meeting could be convened with the pupil's parents, the SENCO, class teacher and other relevant staff to collate information. Prior to the meeting, it is important to gather clear information on which aspects of the child's behaviour or functioning give rise to these concerns and the extent to which strategies to address these have been effectively devised and implemented. Serious thought needs to be given to the type of help and support the child appears to need, how this might be provided and why it is felt that this is not possible within his or her mainstream school. In addition, clear ideas on which other local schools might meet the child's needs better, and why, should be elicited.

It can be all too easy to think that there is the 'perfect school' somewhere else, but the reality is often that this is not the case. Some pupils with an ASD are a challenge to their teachers and their peers, wherever they are educated. In many cases, it is likely that in discussion with parents, staff at the school and outside agencies such as the educational psychologist, outreach teacher or education officer, the conclusion that the child's current mainstream school continues to be the most appropriate placement will be reached, with changes suggested to the pupil's timetable or how he or she is taught, and possibly additional adult support being allocated. Where a change of placement is felt necessary, then a detailed case will need to be presented to the LEA which may lead to a full reassessment of the pupil's needs and ultimately transfer to another school, which might be another mainstream school or a special school or unit.

An alternative to seeking a new 'specialist' placement might be to increase the specialist knowledge of one or more staff at the mainstream school, through training. There are now a number of courses specifically on the education of pupils with an ASD, which lead to a professional qualification. The University of Birmingham, for example, runs campus-based (part-time or full-time) and distance education courses for staff working with pupils with autism leading to a number of qualifications depending on entry skills and length of study (e.g. Advanced Certificate in Education; B.Phil.; M.Ed.). Other universities and colleges of higher education also offer campus-based modules on autistic spectrum disorders. Some of the students are from mainstream settings and others have an outreach role. Many work in special or specialist settings. Accredited courses for support assistants are also available.

Questions on whether a pupil has an autistic spectrum disorder

Staff in mainstream and special schools often ask what they should do if they think that a child might have an autistic spectrum disorder but he or she has not been identified or diagnosed as such. In the first instance, this should be mentioned to the SENCO who will be able to advise on the type of information to collect on the pupil's communication skills, his or her social understanding and behaviour and skills within lessons and at break times. This information could then be discussed and a decision made as to whether to proceed further with the enquiry. If so, the SENCO could raise it with the educational psychologist or the school doctor. Decisions on when and how these concerns are shared with the child's parents will need to be made. The parents could approach their GP, with reports from school and their own observations, for advice and referral on to a child development centre or psychiatric team. If diagnosis of an ASD is made, changes will probably be made to the way in which staff work with the pupil and the priorities they have, in the light of that knowledge, but it is unlikely that the placement itself will need to change. It is also important to bear in mind that autistic spectrum disorders are very variable in their severity and the effects on behaviour; some pupils, even though they may meet the criteria for an ASD, do not have problems in school which require major intervention. Parents of these children may prefer that autism is not a main focus and that the diagnosis is not shared with staff or others; their views should be respected.

Schools are complex systems and it is important that written policies exist on how staff collaborate and work together to address and meet the needs of all pupils on roll. Effective school policies on assessment, behaviour and discipline, bullying, differentiation, special educational needs, parent partnership, and recording and reporting are likely to be particularly important for a pupil with an ASD. Schools are particularly confusing and anxiety-provoking environments and steps need to be taken to minimise this confusion and to lower stress levels for pupils and staff. If staff are clear on procedures and the needs of particular pupils, and feel supported by colleagues and parents, then this will enhance the school life of pupils with an autistic spectrum disorder.

CHAPTER 8

Management of teacher stress

There are a great number of factors currently which have the potential to lead to teacher stress. These include OFSTED inspections, National Curriculum demands and assessments; increasing class sizes, inclusion of more pupils with complex special educational needs; league tables; demands of new initiatives such as the literacy and numeracy hour and the Code of Practice (DfE 1994). So, teaching in a mainstream school is a major challenge in itself and on its own can lead to teacher stress. If, in addition, there are pupils who are very demanding – either in academic terms or in terms of behaviour which is seen as very unusual or challenging – then the level of stress is likely to increase.

Even before starting work with the pupil, teachers can feel a high level of anxiety about the unknown. Starting a job that is unfamiliar is more stress-inducing than working on familiar tasks where competence and confidence have been developed. Having information on ASDs and the 'worst that could happen' in relation to a particular pupil can serve to reduce this anxiety considerably.

Factors which may lead to teacher stress

There are a number of factors which may be challenging and make staff feel deskilled when teaching a pupil with an ASD.

- The fact that the pupil may say or do things which appear to be directed at the teacher personally can lead to feelings that the pupil does not like them or is seeking to undermine staff, which in turn makes staff feel anger or dislike towards the pupil. Staff should remind themselves that difficulty with empathy is a central feature of autism and that the pupil's behaviour rarely has the same intent as similar behaviour from another child.
- The fact that the pupil may not appear to be attending to what the teacher says or to participate in the way staff would want, can lead to feelings that staff are failing, as the pupil does not seem to be enjoying the activity or is not getting anything out of being in the class. Often pupils with an ASD are attending to more of what is going on than they appear to. They seem to be able to observe and to listen to the main event in the classroom while looking out of the window, wandering around the classroom or while engaged in a self-directed activity such

as spinning or twiddling. Staff need to look for other evidence that the pupil is actually learning and benefiting from the activity.

- The fact that they may not respond to the usual incentives to encourage them to do their best work, may lead to feelings of failure and that staff have nothing to excite or interest them; the teacher may think they do not care about their work, as such. What is more likely, is that they are not concerned about other people's opinions about their work or performance as they do not appreciate that other people have thoughts about them. It is possible to find incentives that staff can link with a less desirable activity – as is done with the other pupils – but these rewards may be different from those usually used and need to be identified by the pupil with the ASD.
- The fact that they do not appear to seek out staff approval in the way in which many pupils do, can mean little positive feedback which may lead the teacher to feel rejection and failure.
- They may try very hard to follow their own agenda and seem to reject the plans of the teacher and other pupils – and staff will have to work hard to negotiate and compromise to reach an acceptable outcome for all concerned.
- The fact that there may be particular difficulties for staff when the pupils are asked to work in a pair or groups or to carry out tasks which involve imagining that they are somebody else or in a particular situation, can lead to teachers feeling frustrated and angry if they believe the pupil is being deliberately difficult or opting out.
- The fact that they may start to scream or hit themselves may be frightening to staff and others and lead to feelings of powerlessness as staff are not sure what to do and do not know clearly what the pupil might do next.

So, powerful emotions can be aroused when working with a pupil with an ASD and these can seriously affect the staff's ability to work effectively with them. If staff can read about autism and 'get into the pupil's shoes' and understand how it is the interaction of their autism with their environment that leads them to behave in this way, and not their personal style or competence as a teacher, then feelings of inadequacy will be reduced and stress levels decreased.

A teacher's behaviour towards the pupil and their personal style can serve either to increase the pupil's difficulties or make them feel comfortable at school and enable them to participate effectively in activities and to learn. It is therefore important to be aware of teacher styles and interactions which are likely to lead to positive outcomes for all. The aim is to help the pupil manage in a world that he or she may find difficult to understand and where they feel uncertain as to what to do or say.

Positive outcomes of teaching a pupil with an ASD

Having said all this, there are positive outcomes for the teacher and other staff in working with a pupil with an ASD. To achieve success and develop a relationship with a pupil who does not respond in the usual ways can be very rewarding. Having firsthand experience of a pupil with autism increases our understanding of what it is to be human and how we engage often in behaviours that are wholly designed to 'win and keep' friends, colleagues and family – but which we at times would prefer not to do. Pupils with an ASD sometimes say and do exactly what we would like to, but social conventions and future career prospects advise us against such action. Some of the pupils have skills and knowledge that can be a real asset to the class as a whole. We would argue that once staff have learned how to teach a pupil with an ASD, then they have developed skills and understanding which will help in the teaching of all pupils.

Dealing with stress

Even with an increased understanding of autistic spectrum disorders though, there may be times within the school day that staff feel exhausted, upset and extremely challenged and it is very important to consider how they are going to deal effectively with demands in a way which does not significantly damage their emotional and physical health and well-being. Considerations need to be given to the physical environment, the psychological state of staff and their physical health.

Staff may need to develop strategies to cope with feelings of frustration, fear, anger and anxiety. What is the working environment like? Is it comfortable and attractive for staff and the pupils or is it overcrowded, noisy, hot or cold, with little storage space? Are there aspects which cause difficulties or stress which might be altered? How could staff and others improve on this? How do staff feel most days at school? Factors which contribute to feelings of well-being and the factors which make staff feel despondent or inadequate could be identified. What can staff do to increase the amount of time they feel good?

Self-management of stress

There are a number of ways in which an individual member of staff might ease the pressures on themselves and limit the effects of an upsetting or difficult encounter.

- Think of the situations and times when one feels relaxed and calm. Identify the main characteristics of these and consider how they might be incorporated into life at school.

- Plan times each day during and after school to engage in relaxing and calming activities. Staff may feel they have not got the time, but research shows that after such sessions, one is more productive and efficient and therefore has not actually lost time. Physical exercise can lower anxiety levels and heighten the sense of well-being.

- Pupils also benefit from periods of relaxation and staff can introduce relaxation sessions during the day where lights are dimmed, music is played and oils are burned. This should relax both staff and the pupils.

- Spend time away from the pupils during break times and lunchtimes, in a place where staff can relax.

Support from staff colleagues

A school ethos which encourages staff to share concerns and successes is likely to be conducive to teacher well-being. Staff can provide support to each other in a variety of forms. In terms of professional development, it is helpful to have planned sessions with a senior member of staff to discuss general issues about work within the classroom and the school and to identify strengths and areas of practice to develop. Opportunities for staff to comment positively on each others' work and their contribution to the school can be created.

The school's SENCO has particular responsibility for all pupils with special educational needs at the school, in particular to manage and advise on the Code of Practice procedures. The SENCO can invite staff to discuss concerns about particular pupils, give advice, or seek further advice from within or outside the school. Where support assistants are employed, the SENCO might also convene meetings of all assistants and class teachers to discuss common issues.

Support for support assistants

The personal job satisfaction of a support assistant and their success with a pupil will be largely dependent on the working relationship they develop with classroom teachers. Support assistants often report that they feel an enormous sense of responsibility for the pupil and can find that spending long periods supporting just one pupil emotionally draining and professionally limiting. It is important then to consider ways of varying the work of the assistant. Where the pupil has ten or more hours of support allocated, it may be desirable for this to be provided by more than one adult. A partnership between the teachers and the support assistant that works well can alleviate demands on both and so reduce stress. It is important then that time is given outside classroom hours to discuss how and when both will work with the pupil. There should be regular meetings with the SENCO, the support assistant and other staff to exchange views and discuss any concerns.

Dealing with stressful incidents

The three strategies above relate to planned meetings and discussions. There also needs to be strategies for managing serious events as and when they happen. The more staff understand the pupil and the likely situations which might trigger challenging behaviour, the more staff will be able to pre-empt serious incidents. Discussions on ways to prevent episodes of challenging behaviour are therefore very important and are likely to develop staff confidence and reduce the chances of particularly disruptive behaviour. But, if a pupil does become very distressed, upsets others around him or her, and is difficult to calm, then there needs to be a plan which has been discussed and rehearsed beforehand. If there is no support assistant, then it might be possible to ask a pupil in the class to go for the assistance of a colleague (who should know that he or she might be called upon). If the pupil is hurting a member of staff or other pupils by their actions, then staff have to act in a way that reduces the risk of injury and attempts to calm the pupil. If a member of staff has been hurt, they should not then be the person to support and manage the pupil during and immediately after the incident, if at all possible.

Pupils with an ASD who do not make demands on staff

Working with a pupil with an ASD may not present major management challenges to staff if the pupil is academically able to do the tasks set and poses no real behaviour problems. They may in fact be less demanding than many of the other pupils in the class. The pupil may sit alone in the class and complete their work to a high standard. However, thought needs to be given as to whether they are also developing skills which will be needed for their life in the next phase of their education and ultimately work. They need to be taught strategies to develop their skills in working with others. It is important to observe them in a variety of situations and to discuss school issues with them, in the light of what is known about their difficulties in working within a highly social and often confusing environment. It can be easy to overlook or miss areas of work or leisure time which are not working as well as they might or which are causing real difficulties for the pupil.

As mentioned in Chapter 6, some pupils with an ASD manage to contain all the anxieties and difficulties they experience at school and may be described as 'model pupils', but then when they arrive home, engage in challenging behaviour towards their brothers and sisters or their parents. This is often a reaction to and a release from the stress they have felt under when at school. Discussions with parents about this possibility would be helpful and strategies parents might try when the pupil returns home from school could be explored (e.g. setting up a clear routine for the child to follow, which may involve physical exercise).

Conclusion

Throughout this book, the emphasis has been on trying to understand how pupils with ASDs experience the world and the implications of this for staff within mainstream schools. It has been suggested that it is more helpful and more respectful to the pupils, to view their behaviour as different rather than deficient. Looking for strengths and interests, and working with these, is likely to be more effective than focusing too much on areas which the pupils find very difficult or stressful. The diagnosis of an autistic spectrum disorder should be seen as a signpost to direct staff to the areas which need to be understood, but knowledge of the individual child is crucial.

The educational placement of a child with an ASD has as much to do with LEA and Government policy and the attitude and resources of local schools as it has to do with the characteristics of the child. The attitudes and flexibility of the staff within the schools are major factors in how successful a placement will be. Ideally, staff should receive information and advice on teaching a child with an ASD before that child is placed with them. However, in reality this rarely happens, not just in the case of an individual child entering his or her local mainstream school, but even when a new unit or school is opened specifically for children with an ASD. Many staff have to learn how best to deal with the child 'on the job' and seek advice from sources outside school as and when they can.

It is important that the social and academic demands made on the child are realistic. Taking the line that the pupil must adhere exactly to the same procedures or demands made on others may be counterproductive and unfair, given that the pupil has to manage many additional demands as a result of his or her ASD. Temple Grandin, a very able woman with autism (Sacks 1995), has said that continually trying to work out what to do and what to say is like doing quadratic equations in your head.

There is no magic solution to teaching pupils with ASDs and no staff or setting that will have all the answers. What is important is that staff are prepared to listen and learn (from those with more expertise, including parents and also from the pupil) and to be flexible in their approach. The most important part is the change of attitude, from judgement and fear to openness and concern. Above all, it is important to be committed to eventual success, which will help to ensure that it will be achieved.

References, further reading and useful addresses

References

American Psychiatric Association (1994) *Diagnostic and statistical manual of mental disorders*, 4th edn. Washington DC: American Psychiatric Association.

Barber, C. (1996) 'The integration of a very able pupil with Asperger syndrome into a mainstream school.' *British Journal of Special Education* **23**, 19–24.

Bondy, A. S. and Frost, L. A. (1994) 'The Delaware autistic program', in Harris, S. L. and Handleman, J. S. (eds) *Preschool education programs for children with autism*. Austin: Pro-Ed.

DfE (1994) *Code of Practice on the Identification and Assessment of Special Educational Needs*. London: Department for Education.

Gerland, G. (1997) *A real person: life on the outside*. London: Souvenir Press.

Grandin, T. (1995) 'Cognition', In Schopler, E. and Mesibov, G. B. (eds) *Learning and Cognition in Autism*. New York: Plenum Press.

Jordan, R. and Jones, G. (1996) *Educational provision for children in Scotland: Report of a survey for the SOEID*. Birmingham: School of Education, University of Birmingham.

Jordan, R. and Powell, S. (1990) 'High Scope – a cautionary view', *Early Years* **11**, 29–34.

Jordan, R. and Powell, S. (1995a) 'Factors affecting school choice for parents of a child with autism', *Communication*, Winter, 5–9.

Jordan, R. and Powell, S. (1995b) *Understanding and teaching children with autism*. Chichester: Wiley.

O'Neill, J. L. (1998) 'Autism – isolation not desolation', *Autism: the international journal of research and practice* **2**, 199–204.

Powell, S. and Jordan, R. (1997) 'Rationale for the approach', in Powell, S. and Jordan, R. *Autism and Learning: a guide to good practice*. London: David Fulton Publishers.

Roeyers, H. (1995) 'A peer-mediated proximity intervention to facilitate the social interactions of children with a pervasive developmental disorder', *British Journal of Special Education* **22**, 161–64.

Sacks, O. (1995) *An Anthropologist on Mars*. London: Picador.

Sinclair, J. (1992) 'Bridging the gap: an inside out view of autism', in Schopler, E. and Mesibov, G. (eds) *High functioning individuals with autism*. New York: Plenum Press.

Taylor, G. (1997) 'Community building in schools: developing a circle of friends', *Educational and Child Psychology* **14**, 45–50.

Whitaker, P., *et al.* (1998) 'Children with autism and peer group support', *British Journal of Special Education* 25(2), 60–64.

Williams, D. (1996) *Autism: an inside-out approach.* London: Jessica Kingsley.

Wing, L. (1989) 'The diagnosis of autism', in Gillberg, C. (ed) *Diagnosis and Treatment of Autism.* New York: Plenum Press.

Wing, L. (1996) *The Autistic Spectrum.* London: Constable.

World Health Organisation (1992) *International classification of diseases, 10th revision.* Geneva: WHO.

Further reading

Attwood, T. (1997) *Asperger syndrome: a guide for parents and professionals.* London: Jessica Kingsley.

Cumine, V., Leach, J. and Stevenson, G. (1997) *Asperger syndrome: a practical guide for teachers.* London: David Fulton Publishers.

Davies, J. (1993) *Children with autism: a booklet for brothers and sisters.* Nottingham: Early Years Centre, Ravenshead, Notts.

Davies, J. (1993) *Children with Asperger syndrome: a booklet for brothers and sisters.* Nottingham: Early Years Centre, Ravenshead, Notts.

Leicestershire County Council and Fosse Health Trust (1998) *Autism: how to help your young child.* London: National Autistic Society.

Leicestershire County Council and Fosse Health Trust (1998) *Asperger syndrome: a guide for teachers.* London: National Autistic Society.

Powell, S. and Jordan, R. (1997) *Autism and Learning: a guide to good practice.* London: David Fulton Publishers.

Useful addresses

Circles Network
Pamwell House, 160 Pennywell Road, Easton, Bristol B55 0TX
Telephone: 0117 9393917

National Autistic Society
393 City Road, London, EC1V 1NE
Telephone: 0171 833 2299

Index